Grammar Rules!

High-Interest Activities for Practice
and Mastery of Basic
Grammar Skills

Grades 5-6

▶ by Jillayne Prince Wallaker

▶ Dedication

With lots of love to Maegen, Madalen, Ian, and always to Willie.

▶ Credits

Editors:
Tracy Soles, Donna Walkush

Layout Design:
Victory Productions, Inc.

Illustrations:
Janet Armbrust

Cover Design:
Peggy Jackson

ISBN 0-88724-977-9

▶ Contents

▶ Contents

▶ Introduction

Some might be surprised by the title *Grammar Rules!* However, this grammar book was developed so that writing teachers can show students that grammar can be understood (and sometimes even fun) when presented in a clear, reasonable way. *Grammar Rules!* builds on each topic in a logical progression so that students learn the facts behind the skill, practice the skill, then are able to put their new grammar knowledge into action.

After each grammar skill is introduced, plenty of practice is provided, along with a Review Work and a Draft Book exercise for students to transfer their new skill. Review Work assignments focus on previously covered skills or provides additional practice with a skill on the given page. The Draft Book assignments encourage students to apply the grammar skills beyond the reproducible pages and incorporate them into their own writing. For the Draft Book activities, students can complete assignments on loose-leaf paper in a folder or in a spiral or composition notebook.

Each grammar skill presented in the Review Work and Draft Book exercises has a locator code, such as underlining nouns with yellow. This code is consistent throughout the series. This provides a student with a patterned tool for self-monitoring as well as self-editing.

This book also contains a comprehensive review on pages 112-114. These pages are perfect for a pre- and post-assessment or an end-of-year test.

A student editing checklist is included on page 115. This page is designed to be used as a self-editing tool. By assigning two or three items to check at a time, students are not overwhelmed with "getting everything right," but instead can focus on very specific skills until they understand them completely. Once mastery of the selected editing skills is evident, an additional set of items can be assigned. The same piece of student writing can be used for several editing assignments or students can use different writing samples. This convenient checklist can be kept with student Draft Books as a reminder of grammatical variations that can be included in their writing. It can also be used to monitor student progress by dating each skill when it is demonstrated consistently.

Grammar Rules! will quickly become a resource that writing teachers return to for strong grammar activities to show their students that grammar really does rule!

Name _____

▶ Rocks

The main parts of speech include the following: nouns, verbs, pronouns, adjectives, adverbs, and conjunctions.

Write the part of speech for each numbered word on the line.

(1)Arnie studies rocks and minerals with his class. The class observes rocks, performs field tests on the minerals, and reads extensively about both. He discovered that there are three (2)types of rocks: sedimentary, igneous, and metamorphic.

Sedimentary rocks are formed in layers. The layers are deposited in streams and riverbeds. Sand, pebbles, plant matter, and (3)animal parts can all end up in these layers. Over time, the layers (4)solidify, and sedimentary rock is formed. The (5)plant matter and animal parts become fossils.

Igneous rocks are formed in, under, and around volcanoes. The molten rock, or heated liquid rock, forms underground. (6)It is called magma. Some magma cools (7)slowly underground, becoming igneous rock. Pressure causes other magma to rise to the surface. When magma (8)exits the volcano, its name changes to lava. Lava flows from the volcano, incinerating everything it touches. (9)Finally, it cools. (10)Solidified lava is igneous rock. Igneous rocks have many different looks depending on how (11)quickly they cool. Igneous rock can have air bubbles and be very light, (12)or it can be jet black and very solid.

Metamorphic rock is changed rock. It (13)forms deep underground. Sedimentary or igneous rock that has been compressed by underground pressure (14)and heat becomes metamorphic rock. The heat and pressure cause the layers of sedimentary and igneous rock to become meshed together, much like the cheese in a grilled-cheese sandwich meshes (15)slightly with the bread on each side.

(16)These three rock types are the literal (17)building blocks of Earth. (18)They provide stability to our structures and provide many building materials for the items (19)we use daily. Arnie finds rocks (20)fascinating.

1. _____
2. _____
3. _____
4. _____
5. _____
6. _____
7. _____
8. _____
9. _____
10. _____
11. _____
12. _____
13. _____
14. _____
15. _____
16. _____
17. _____
18. _____
19. _____
20. _____

🔍 Review Work

Underline 10 nouns in this piece of writing with yellow.

✏️ Draft Book

Locate a piece of your writing. Underline nouns with yellow. Underline verbs with blue.

Name _____

▶ Categories

Nouns are words that name people, places, things, or ideas.

Underline the nouns in the sentences. Write each noun in the correct category below.

Norman vacations on a peninsula in Maine.

Kangaroos live in Australia.

The crowd clapped and cheered.

Carma studied flowering plant pollen.

Those mittens belong to Melanie.

Elle, Neil, and Miss Kent went to the tennis courts.

The bird in that cage belongs to Iris.

Their family went to Oregon.

The rabbit left tracks in the snow in our yard.

The cafeteria in our school is great.

People: _____

_____

Places: _____

_____

Things: _____

_____

 Review Work

Draw an X next to each proper noun that names a person. Draw a triangle above each proper noun that names a place.

 Draft Book

Make lists of people you know, places you have been, and things that interest you. Write 10 nouns for each list. Use these nouns in future writing assignments.

Name _____

They Are Special

common and proper nouns

Proper nouns name specific people, places, things, or ideas. A person's first and last names are proper nouns, as well as titles like Mr., Mrs., Miss, Dr., etc. A proper noun always begins with an uppercase letter. All other nouns are common nouns. A common noun does not begin with an uppercase letter.

For each proper noun, cross out the lowercase letter and write the uppercase letter above it. Put an uppercase letter at the beginning of each sentence.

frédéric auguste bartholdi, a frenchman, designed the statue of liberty.

the pentagon is in arlington, virginia.

mackinac bridge connects the upper and lower parts of michigan.

in philadelphia, you can see the liberty bell and visit independence hall.

arches national park in utah has famous rock spires and stone spans.

brandon, julio, and carlos are hiking near paulina peak.

Write a proper noun for each common noun.

People

teacher: _____   student: _____

adult: _____   doctor: _____

Places

state: _____   restaurant: _____

school: _____   continent: _____

Things

toy: _____   food: _____

animal: _____   book: _____

Review Work

Underline common nouns in the sentences with yellow.

Draft Book

Write five sentences using proper nouns.
Underline each noun with yellow. Capitalize the proper nouns.

▶ He, She, or It ▶ gender nouns

Gender is the sex referred to by a noun. The English language has four genders: masculine (male), feminine (female), neuter (no sex), and indefinite (either sex).

Circle the indefinite nouns.

classmates	niece	team	ducks	mare	student	nephew	siblings
mail carrier	people	aunt	relatives	queen	animals	parents	prince
champion	friend	milk	player	book	singer	umbrella	pencil

Write the underlined nouns in the proper categories. Add two of your own nouns to each category.

A <u>knight</u> in shining <u>armor</u> saved the <u>princess</u> from the <u>dragon</u>.

My <u>grandmother</u> is a <u>doctor</u>, and my <u>uncle</u> is a <u>nurse</u>.

Our <u>cousins</u> have <u>roosters</u> and <u>hens</u> in a <u>coop</u>.

The <u>king</u> wanted the <u>jester</u> to do <u>tricks</u> and sing <u>songs</u>.

Her <u>sister</u> and <u>brother</u> roasted <u>hot dogs</u> and <u>marshmallows</u>.

Masculine: _____

_____

Feminine: _____

_____

Neuter: _____

_____

Indefinite: _____

_____

🔍 Review Work

Draw an X above each noun in the sentences that names a person.

✏️ Draft Book

Write two sentences for each noun category. Above each noun, indicate the gender: M = masculine, F = feminine, N = neuter, or I = indefinite.

Name _____

▶ I'll Take These Plural ▶ plural nouns

A plural noun is a noun that names more than one person, place, thing, or idea.

Usually, add an *s* to make a noun plural: cat + s = cats
If a singular noun ends in *ch, s, z, sh,* or *x,* add *es*: patch + es = patches
If a noun ends in *f* or *fe*, change *f* or *fe* to *v* and add *es*: life + es = lives
If a noun ends in a consonant + *y*, change the *y* to *i* and add *es* :
    party + es = parties
If a noun ends in a vowel + *y* or a vowel + *o*, add *s*: boy + s = boys
If a noun ends in a consonant + *o*, add *es*: tomato + es = tomatoes

Write the plural form of each singular noun.

stereo	_____	sandwich	_____
buzz	_____	crash	_____
match	_____	ax	_____
wife	_____	calf	_____
thief	_____	radio	_____
elf	_____	lady	_____
country	_____	city	_____
guppy	_____	jelly	_____
hobby	_____	strawberry	_____
pass	_____	chimney	_____
boy	_____	toy	_____
bay	_____	turkey	_____
domino	_____	potato	_____
hero	_____	video	_____

🔍 Review Work

Draw a star next to each person and place noun.

✏️ Draft Book

Choose 10 noun pairs (singular and plural forms). Write a sentence for each noun.

▶ Tricky Nouns ▷ irregular plural nouns

Some nouns change in the middles or ends when they become plural. Others do not change when they become plural.

examples (change): axis ⟶ axes   medium ⟶ media
examples (no change): bison, deer, moose, series, sheep, swine

Match the singular and plural nouns. Write the number in front of the singular noun in the box in front of the correct plural noun.

1. goose
2. phenomenon
3. hippopotamus
4. mouse
5. tooth
6. cactus
7. child
8. foot
9. person
10. louse
11. octopus
12. man
13. woman
14. die
15. ox

☐ phenomena
☐ teeth
☐ children
☐ feet
☐ people
☐ men
☐ cacti
☐ geese
☐ oxen
☐ octopuses
☐ dice
☐ hippopotamuses
☐ lice
☐ women
☐ mice

Review Work

Write the plural form of the following nouns:

flower _____ crisis _____ pitcher _____ life _____

Draft Book

Write a story using some of the tricky nouns on this page. Circle the plural nouns. Draw a star next to each singular noun.

Name _____

▶ Mine, All Mine

A possessive noun shows belonging. If a noun is singular or if it is plural but does not end with an *s*, add an apostrophe + *s* to the end to make it possessive.

example: cat's food, boss's pen, men's belts

If a noun is plural and already ends with an *s*, add an apostrophe to the end.

example: cats' collars, dancers' shoes

Change the following ownership phrases into phrases using possessive nouns.

the toys belonging to the brothers   _____

the brush belonging to Iris   _____

the ball belonging to the twins   _____

the bike belonging to his sister   _____

the pencil belonging to Mrs. Fris   _____

the pillow belonging to Adam   _____

the score book belonging to the team   _____

Circle each possessive noun. Write *SP* if it is singular possessive or *PP* if it is plural possessive.

_____ The dog's new, leather collar is lost.

_____ The snails' aquarium needed cleaning.

_____ The art project's colors were faded by the sun.

_____ We peeked into the teachers' lounge.

_____ Carlos borrowed Millie's new crayons.

_____ The dancers' audience clapped wildly.

_____ The children's balloons blew away.

Review Work

Underline the plural nouns with yellow.

Draft Book

Write 10 sentences using possessive nouns. Include both singular possessive and plural possessive nouns.

Name _____

▶ Action

An action verb is a word that tells what someone or something is doing.
> **example:** The boy **swims** at the beach.

Circle each verb.

A jar of fireflies provides nearly enough light to read by.

Scientists used a spectrometer to learn more about solar light.

Fluffy scrambled eggs melt in your mouth.

Tolan filled the colander with apples.

Silkworms spin cocoons of silk thread.

Water condenses on icy glasses in the summer.

Rita tumbled down the sand dune.

Adele and I designed a cultural outfit.

George swings the golf club.

The cat claws the furniture.

Nellie calculates the total.

Butterflies flutter from one flower to another.

Danielle shivers without her coat and hat.

The table-tennis ball bounced across the table.

Sal and Marshall snorkel in the bay.

 Review Work

> Write an *N* above each neuter noun.

 Draft Book

> Find a page of writing in your Draft Book with the nouns underlined with yellow.
> Underline the verbs with blue.

► Lunch in the Inlet ▸ action verbs

An action verb is a word that tells what someone or something is doing.

Fill in the blanks with verbs from the list or choose your own. Use each word only once.

appears	captures	cruises	devours	glides
gulps	scouts	shines	sift	slides
slips	snags	snaps	teems	sits

The inlet _____ calm and quiet.

Below, the murky water _____ with life.

A crayfish _____ at a passing minnow.

The minnow _____ small water organisms.

A pike _____ its territory.

His meal _____ right across his path.

Ducks _____ along the surface of the water.

Duck bills _____ through the mud looking for treats.

A little, green frog _____ on a lily pad.

The frog _____ a fly buzzing just out of reach.

A snake _____ into the water eyeing the unwary frog.

The snake _____ the frog.

A turtle _____ off a log.

The sun _____ down beginning a lazy afternoon.

🔍 Review Work

Write an *I* above each indefinite pronoun.

✏️ Draft Book

Find a page of your writing in your Draft Book or write
a story about what happens in the cafeteria during lunch.
Underline the nouns with yellow and the verbs with blue.

Name _____

 # Give a Helping Hand > helping verbs/ verb phrases

Helping verbs are verbs that help main verbs express tense. There are 23 helping verbs. A verb phrase acts as a single verb and is made of a main verb with one or more helping verbs. Up to three helping verbs can precede the main verb. *Would, should, shall,* and *will* are helping verbs. Forms of the following verbs are also helping verbs:

be: am, are, is, was, were, be, being, been
do: do, does, did
have: have, has, had
may: may, must, might
can: can, could

Circle the helping verbs. Underline the verb phrases.

The fleas did jump through the cat's fur.

The water is pouring into the basement.

The ant had scurried into the anthill.

We are going to the amusement park.

I am excited to be here.

The lights can be dimmed with this switch.

Max was entitled to his turn.

The puppy must have tried to jump onto the bed.

That jam would make a good ice-cream topping.

The bird had flown into the bushes.

We should weed the garden before it gets too hot.

The tickets may cost too much.

Emma's family might go to the zoo tomorrow.

 ## Review Work

Underline the nouns with yellow.

 ## Draft Book

Write 10 sentences that use helping verbs. Circle the helping verbs. Underline the verb phrases with blue.

Name _____

▶ Link Them Together > linking verbs

A linking verb is a verb that does not show action. It links or joins something in the predicate to the rest of the sentence. It does not have an action verb after it.

Forms of the verb *to be* are the most common linking verbs. There are eight forms of the verb *to be*: *am, are, is, was, were,* (*will*) *be,* (*am, are, was, were*) *being,* (*have, has, had*) *been.* Other linking verbs include forms of these verbs: *to appear, to become, to feel, to grow, to look, to remain, to seem, to smell, to sound,* and *to taste.*

Underline the linking verbs.

The knitted mittens are very warm.

The food on the table appears appetizing.

The neighbor's dog, who was sprayed by a skunk, smells awful.

The garbage can by the door is full.

That frozen drink tastes fruity.

The lilac bushes, planted when I was born, grow more beautiful every year.

Haley, April's big sister, is our junior counselor.

Amber, my younger cousin, will be in first grade next year.

The moon was like a huge orange ball hovering in the sky.

The music, which played for hours, grew increasingly louder.

Ms. Tolio, my mom's friend, is a pediatric neurosurgeon.

Mom's new scissors are sharp enough to cut corrugated cardboard.

Mr. Grogan, my orthodontist, is nice.

Last night Venus was visible low in the sky.

🔍 Review Work

Draw a star above each person noun.

✏ Draft Book

Write 10 sentences that use linking verbs. Use a variety of the linking verbs listed above. Underline the linking verbs with blue.

Name _____

▶ Choose the Verb

noun and verb agreement

A singular noun uses a verb with an *s* at the end. A plural noun uses a verb that does not have an *s* at the end.

examples: The **boy climbs** the tree.
The **boys climb** the tree.

A verb uses the same rules as a noun when adding *s* or *es*.

Usually, add an *s* to a verb: run + s = runs
If a verb ends in *sh, s, z, ch,* or *x*, add *es*: pitch + es = pitches
If a verb ends in a consonant + *y*, change *y* to *i* and add *es*: try - y + i + es = tries
If a verb ends in a vowel + *y*, add *s*: enjoy + s = enjoys

Circle the correct verbs.

Blair (stare, stares) at the massive mess in her room.

Jade and I (catch, catches) outfield balls.

Students (choose, chooses) which vegetables to eat.

Numerous plants (thrive, thrives) in the rain forest.

People (access, accesses) the Internet.

Not many minnows (survive, survives) to become adult fish.

Darryl (complain, complains) about mowing the lawn.

Squirrels (flee, flees) when my sister opens the sliding door.

Santos (invite, invites) his friends to a sleepover.

Juan and Doug (agree, agrees) on the answer.

Our kites (fly, flies) through the air at the beach.

Mother (half, halves) the candy bar for us to share.

Kara (spread, spreads) jelly onto the peanut butter sandwich.

🔍 Review Work

Draw an X above each proper noun in the sentences that names a person.

✏ Draft Book

Choose five of the sentences. Rewrite each one so that the first noun is the opposite (singular or plural) of what it is now. Rewrite the verb to agree with the new subject.

CD-4339 Grammar Rules! Grades 5–6   **17**

LC 1.2

Name _____

▶ Subjects

The simple subject of a sentence is the noun that the sentence is about.

example: Pat's **fish** swam in the aquarium.

example: Mount Everest is the tallest mountain in the world.

Underline the noun that is the simple subject of each sentence.

Most tree branches grow at an acute angle from the tree trunk.

The penny rolled under the cabinet.

Chan's watch was slow by an hour.

The thermometer read 62 degrees Fahrenheit.

The Marianas Trench is deeper than Mount Everest is tall.

Mount Rushmore towers over the valley.

The praying mantis is related to the cockroach.

My mom made homemade strawberry jam.

Ladybugs assist farmers by eating harmful insects.

Garnet is the January birthstone.

Abigail vacationed in California.

Parrots require lots of attention.

Bamboo is not a tree.

Paul teased Talia about the food in her lunch.

 Review Work

Circle the plural nouns.

Draft Book

Find a full page of writing in your Draft Book or write a story about your favorite hobby or sport. Write an *SS* above the simple subject in each sentence.

Name _____

▶ Fill in the Subject ▷ simple subject of a sentence

The simple subject of a sentence is the noun that the sentence is about.

example: Anna's **bike** is red.

example: **Mount Rushmore** required years of effort to construct.

Add a simple subject to each sentence by using a singular or plural noun as indicated. If a proper noun is used, capitalize it.

singular   A _____ can be used for drawing.

singular   _____ is an ingredient of this meal.

plural   Many _____ grow on trees.

singular   The little _____ crawled across the picnic table.

plural   _____ can destroy homes.

plural   Gerard's remote-controlled _____ are awesome.

singular   The _____ hovered over the red flower.

plural   _____ are great places to visit.

singular   The _____ is in the backyard.

plural   The _____ disagree about everything.

singular   A large _____ works well for this task.

plural   _____ eat only plants.

singular   _____ is my favorite park.

plural   _____ are great to read.

singular   An _____ is a healthy snack.

plural   Those _____ should be washed.

🔍 Review Work

Underline the nouns that are not simple subjects with yellow.

✏️ Draft Book

Find a full page of writing in your Draft Book. Write an *SS* above the simple subject in each sentence.

Name _____

▶ Pick the Pronoun ⟩ subject pronouns

A pronoun takes the place of a noun. Subject pronouns take the place of simple subject nouns. They are *I, you, he, she, we, they,* and *it.*

Above each set of nouns, write the pronoun that could take each word's place. Add four nouns to each list.

_____

peninsula	_____
monorail	_____
dog	_____
television	_____

_____

Aunt Amy	_____
Darla	_____
Mrs. Stamey	_____
Mother	_____

_____

the choir	_____
Tim and Meg	_____
the team	_____
the customers	_____

_____

George and I	_____
my brother and I	_____
my class and I	_____
you and I	_____

_____

Mr. Foote	_____
the king	_____
Uncle Joe	_____
Tom	_____

Replace the words in bold type with subject pronouns. Write the correct pronoun on each line.

Ken removed the fender and repaired it. _____

The moon is full and bright tonight. _____

Gary and I invented a new sandwich. _____

Raccoons raided our garbage can. _____

Mrs. Berrier gave us a pop quiz today. _____

 Review Work

Underline the nouns in the sentences above with yellow.

 Draft Book

Find a page of writing in your Draft Book. Change the subject nouns to subject pronouns.

▶ Doing What?

simple predicate

The simple predicate is the main verb of the sentence that tells what someone or something is doing.

Underline each simple predicate.

San panicked when he noticed his lunch money missing.

The aurora borealis shimmered across the night sky.

Monarch caterpillars devour milkweed leaves.

Mosquitoes transmit malaria.

Crystie grabbed the swing with both hands.

The monkey turned around.

Rick bowled his fifth strike in a row.

The roller coaster catapulted its riders forward.

Tears poured from their eyes.

Annie and Sarah gathered the blankets.

Dean completed the order form.

He soaked them with the hose.

Mr. Roark answered their questions.

Mannie and I counted the money.

 Review Work

Write an *SS* above the simple subject in each sentence.

 Draft Book

Use one of the sentences on this page in a story. Underline the simple predicates with blue.

▶ The Animal World

simple subjects and predicates

The simple subject of a sentence is the noun that the sentence is about. The simple predicate is the verb that tells what someone or something is doing.

Underline each simple subject once. Underline each simple predicate twice.

An owl watches.

Worms burrow.

An orca surfaces.

Moths flutter.

An elephant trumpets.

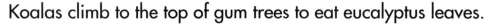

The spider on the web captures an unwary fly.

The gazelles stampede across the plains.

Koalas climb to the top of gum trees to eat eucalyptus leaves.

The soaring hawk scans the land for small rodents.

A red fox slinks through the underbrush towards the rabbit.

Write the plural nouns with their verbs.

_____   _____

_____   _____

Write the singular nouns with their verbs.

_____   _____

_____   _____

_____   _____

 **Review Work**

Underline the other nouns in the sentences with yellow.

Draft Book

Begin a verb list. Record interesting verbs for use in future writing assignments.

Name _____

▶ It Happened Before   ▶ past tense

Tense tells time. It informs the reader when the sentence takes place. If the action happened in the past, it is past tense. There are several ways to make a verb past tense.

    Usually, add *ed* or *d* to a verb: box + ed = boxed, wave + d = waved

    If a verb ends with a consonant + *y*, change *y* to *i* and add *ed*:
    carry - y + i + ed = carried.

    If a verb has a short vowel with one consonant, double the consonant then add *ed*: tip + p + ed = tipped, stop + p + ed = stopped.

Use the rules above to make the verbs past tense.

rustle   _____   end   _____

bat   _____   cry   _____

splatter   _____   trip   _____

agree   _____   snap   _____

ship   _____   create   _____

Write the correct past tense verb on each line.

Julio (copy) _____ his work onto clean paper.

The kitten (pounce) _____ on the ladybug.

Quincy (try) _____ spinach for the first time.

The firefighter (parachute) _____ into the fire zone.

Paulo (hurry) _____ to his piano lesson.

Annabelle (play) _____ with her cousin.

Brett (shop) _____ for new shoes.

Review Work

Write an *SS* above the simple subject in each sentence.

Draft Book

Choose five verb pairs (present and past tense). Write two sentences for each verb. Use the present tense verb in one sentence and the past tense verb in the other.

▶ Now or Then

Tense tells time. When it happened in the past, it is past tense. When something happens now, it is present tense.

Underline the verb in each first sentence. Write the past tense of the verb in each second sentence.

Children crawl through the obstacle course.

Yesterday, they _____ through by the hundreds.

Mosquitoes bother the horses.

They _____ the dogs last week.

Hector bounces on the trampoline.

He _____ on it with Andy earlier.

Meg and I roll the cookie dough very carefully.

We _____ enough dough to make six dozen cookies.

The doctor inoculates the child.

She _____ several children this morning.

Tara and Nell drift along on the inner tubes.

They _____ downstream.

The news helicopter hovers over the scene.

It _____ there until the photos were taken.

Mark tastes the broccoli salad.

He _____ the artichoke dip earlier.

🔍 Review Work

Underline the subject nouns in the first sentences with yellow. Underline the pronouns that replaced them in the second sentences with red.

✏️ Draft Book

Find a story you wrote in your Draft Book. Put boxes around verbs with *ed* endings.

LCI.2

Name _____

▶ Now and Then

Tense tells time. It informs the reader when the sentence takes place. One way to make a verb past tense is to add *ed* to the end.

    past tense: Sam **studied** for the test.

    present tense: Sam **studies** for the test.

An irregular verb becomes past tense by changing its spelling.

    example: catch/caught, shine/shone, sting/stung

Circle the simple predicate. Identify the tense of the verb by writing *past* or *present* on the line.

Bees buzz around the daisies.

Maddie brushes sand from her legs.

Kali ate ice cream.

The parakeet nibbled on crackers.

Fiona bandages the cut on her knee.

Cameron sharpened his pencils for the test.

Kris disturbs the teacher.

Brad and Jeremy left the theater.

The hamsters race around their cages.

Andy wrote a great acrostic poem.

Sally photographs our field trips.

My brother taught me to tie my shoes.

Willie shovels sand into the sandbox.

Jennifer threw hay into the horse stalls.

Dillon cried for his bottle.

 Review Work

    Write an *SS* above each simple subject.

 Draft Book

    Write five sentences using present tense verbs and five sentences using past tense verbs.

Name _____

▶ Things to Come ▶ future tense

Tense tells time. It informs the reader when the sentence takes place. To make a verb future tense, add the helping verb *will* before the singular present tense form of the verb. If the verb has an ending, drop it before adding *will*.

example: Bob **rakes** the lawn. Bob **will rake** the lawn.
Jan **ate** the apple. Jan **will eat** the apple.

Write the correct future tense verb on each line.

Jeremy (builds) _____ a birdhouse.

Allie (caught) _____ some fish.

The boat (cruises) _____ around the channel.

Blake and Rico (jumped) _____ into the pool.

The class (observes) _____ the plants as they grow.

Jess (painted) _____ that set of chairs.

The monkey (grabbed) _____ the rope.

Quinn (helped) _____ make the cake.

Sydney (completed) _____ the book.

A dolphin (bumps) _____ the boat gently.

Jordi (brought) _____ cupcakes for the party.

The sauce (burns) _____ with the burner on high.

Sukie (carries) _____ the blueberries to the car.

Ian, Marshall, and Jacob (threw) _____ water balloons.

The silverware (clatters) _____ to the floor.

 Review Work

Underline the nouns with yellow.

Draft Book

Write about an imaginary trip using future tense verbs.

LC1.2

Name _____

Verbs use tenses to tell when something is happening.

Underline the verbs. If a verb is future tense, underline both the main verb and the helping verb _will_. Circle past, present, or future.

The barrel collects rainwater.	past	present	future
Jamie writes to her friend.	past	present	future
Layne will microwave the popcorn.	past	present	future
Jackie planted the garden.	past	present	future
Marco will arrange the flowers.	past	present	future
The soup boiled over onto the stove.	past	present	future
Chris will lounge in the hammock.	past	present	future
The saw cut through the tree limb.	past	present	future
The driver backed into the parking space.	past	present	future
Hailey slapped the card onto the table.	past	present	future
The chef prepares dinner.	past	present	future
The jellyfish will float on the waves.	past	present	future
Meg pesters her sister.	past	present	future
Ernie will bait the hook.	past	present	future
Nell will chew the strawberry bubble gum.	past	present	future
Maddie and Deb manipulate the controls.	past	present	future
Rich searched for frogs and crayfish in the pond.	past	present	future

 Review Work

Underline the nouns with yellow.

 Draft Book

Write two sentences for each verb tense.
Underline the verbs with blue. Label the sentences past, present, or future tense.

LCL.2

▶ Regular Describers   adjectives

Adjectives are words that describe nouns. Adjectives tell what kind, how many, or which one. They can include number, color, size, shape, or other detail words.

examples: The **dirty** puppy needs a bath.   The **public** library is closed today.

A sentence can have more than one adjective.

example: Four, gray bugs are in the **small** garden.

Circle the adjectives. Draw an arrow from each adjective to the noun it describes.

A wood-handled shovel leaned against the old, red wheelbarrow.

The filthy refrigerator needed to be scoured.

I have mint gum in my top drawer.

The new purple pen is leaking ink.

Five colorful birds swooped through the warm air.

A tired Pete found muddy footprints on the clean floor.

A riderless skateboard zoomed down the steep hill.

Alicia jumped into the cool pool water.

The itchy bumps were not bug bites.

The glowing coals were ready to cook the raw hamburger.

Grandma gave us cherry pie with vanilla ice cream.

An uncooperative child threw an enormous fit in the restaurant.

🔍 **Review Work**

Underline the simple predicates twice.

 Draft Book

Write 10 sentences that have adjectives in them. Circle each adjective. Draw an arrow from the adjective to the noun it describes.

Name _____

▶ Other Describers ▶ demonstrative and common adjectives

Adjectives are words that describe nouns. Adjectives tell what kind, how many, or which one. They can include number, color, size, shape, or other detail words. The four demonstrative adjectives that answer which one are: *this*, *that*, *these*, and *those*. Common adjectives are regular adjectives.

Circle the adjectives. Draw an arrow from each adjective to the noun it describes.

Those scented candles produce very hot wax.

That four-year-old child chatters constantly.

This fuzzy peach has a bruised spot.

Those majestic glaciers tower above this cruise ship.

That dirty blue sock has a small hole in the toe.

This yellow pencil has a broken point.

My little sister is in that class.

Barney wants that chocolate cupcake with white frosting.

Vera drew that seaside sketch with the thunderous storm clouds.

These tiny black seeds can grow delicious white radishes.

Those glass marbles belong to that boy.

That black camera takes great photographs.

 Review Work

Write a *D* above each demonstrative adjective.

 Draft Book

Write 10 sentences that have adjectives in them. Circle each adjective. Draw an arrow from the adjective to the noun it describes.

▶ Special Describers ▶ proper adjectives

Adjectives are words that describe nouns. The four demonstrative adjectives are: *this*, *that*, *these*, and *those*. Common adjectives are regular adjectives. Proper adjectives are made from proper nouns. They are always capitalized. However, the nouns they modify are usually not capitalized. Some proper adjectives are spelled the same as the proper nouns.

example: Mom has **Idaho** potatoes and **Empire** apples on that shelf.

Other proper adjectives have different spellings than the proper nouns.

example: noun: Switzerland   adjective: Swiss
            noun: China   adjective: Chinese

Underline the nouns. Circle the proper adjectives.

The luxury car's seats were made of Italian leather.

Ben ordered New England clam chowder and Maine lobsters.

William Shakespeare is a famous English playwright.

Koe wore her Japanese kimono for the festival.

Did you see the Chinese dragon on the menu cover?

Rhyan's family observes the Jewish tradition of lighting the menorah.

The Canadian roads were lined with trees.

Sydney is a coastal Australian city.

Many unusual creatures live in Brazilian rain forests.

The Egyptian exhibit at the museum was filled with interesting artifacts.

◯ Review Work

Draw an arrow from each proper adjective to the noun it describes.

✎ Draft Book

Write 10 sentences that have adjectives in them. Include proper, demonstrative, and common adjectives. Circle each adjective and draw an arrow to the noun it describes.

▶ Choose Your Adjective ⟩ adjectives

Adjectives are words that describe nouns. The four demonstrative adjectives are: *this*, *that*, *these*, and *those*. Common adjectives, like common nouns, are not capitalized. Proper adjectives are made from proper nouns. They are always capitalized. However, the nouns they modify are not usually capitalized.

Underline the nouns. Circle the proper adjectives. Draw an arrow from each proper adjective to the noun it describes.

That New York cheesecake is absolutely delicious.

Zoe studied about Roman emperors for her social studies test.

The Arctic region is home to little, white, baby harp seals.

Abby made an acute angle on that triangle.

We are eating Mexican food for dinner tonight.

Those noisy birds woke up the entire neighborhood.

Nena went to a Michigan zoo to see the cute Australian koalas.

Owen parked his green mountain bike next to that chain-link fence.

The best bodysurfers around are the California sea lions.

My grandmother has an Austrian crystal on her oak shelf.

My Irish relatives hosted a St. Patrick's Day party this year.

🔍 Review Work

Write a *D* above each demonstrative adjective.

✎ Draft Book

Write 10 sentences that have adjectives in them. Include proper, demonstrative, and common adjectives. Circle each adjective. Draw an arrow from the adjective to the noun it describes.

▶ At the End

adjectives: positive, comparative, superlative

Adjectives describe and/or compare nouns. There are three degrees of comparison. The positive degree describes a noun (or nouns). The comparative degree compares two nouns (add *er* or the words *more* or *less*). The superlative degree compares more than two nouns (add *est* or the words *most* or *least*).

Usually, comparative and superlative adjectives are formed by adding the suffixes *er* and *est* with no changes to the base words. There are some exceptions.

If an adjective ends with *e*, drop the *e* and add *er* or *est*: rare + est = rarest.

If an adjective ends in a consonant + *y*, change *y* to *i* and add *er* or *est*: funny - y + er = funnier.

If an adjective has a short vowel with one consonant, double the consonant then add *er* or *est*: mad + d + er = madder.

If an adjective has two or more syllables, use *more, most, less,* or *least* in front of it.

Add *er* and *est* to each adjective to make the comparative and superlative forms.

Positive	Comparative	Superlative
angry	_____	_____
wise	_____	_____
fast	_____	_____
great	_____	_____

Add *more* and *most* to each adjective to make the comparative and superlative forms.

Positive	Comparative	Superlative
delicious	_____	_____
interesting	_____	_____
vibrant	_____	_____
majestic	_____	_____

🔍 Review Work

Write the comparative and superlative forms of the following adjectives: lucky, delightful, tame, sad, old.

✏️ Draft Book

Write 10 sentences using comparative and superlative forms of adjectives.

Name _____

▶ -Er or More ▷ adjectives: positive, comparative, superlative

Usually, comparative and superlative adjectives are formed by adding *er* and *est*, but for a few adjectives, the spelling must be changed. Comparative and superlative adjectives can also be formed by adding the comparison words *more, most, less,* or *least*. However, when using the comparative and superlative forms of an adjective do not precede the adjective with these words.

example: Don is smarter. (yes)
Don is more smarter. (no)
Don is most smarter. (no)

Circle the correct adjectives.

The (nearest, more nearest) restaurant is four miles away.

This hot chocolate is (hotter, most hot) than I like it.

My friend Pedro is the (most nicer, nicest) person I know.

That movie is (more interesting, interestinger) than the one we watched last week.

This book is (less intenser, less intense) than its sequel.

This assignment is (harder, more harder) than yesterday's was.

The (best, more best) hot dogs are those toasted on an open fire.

My parents are the (least happy, least happier) when I get home late.

That batch of applesauce is (sweeter, more sweeter) than this batch.

Your head is (more protecteder, more protected) with a bike helmet.

We tasted the (more worst, worst) lunch in history today.

The (most gigantic, most giganticest) spider ever just crawled across the floor.

The (older, more older) basketball is the (more better, better) ball.

Review Work

Write an SS above the simple subject in each sentence.

Draft Book

Write 10 sentences using comparative and superlative forms of adjectives.

▶ Odd Adjectives

present and past participles

A participle is a verb form. It acts as an adjective. The present participle is the *ing* form of a verb. The past participle usually ends in *d* or *ed*.

examples: The **crying** baby was hungry.　　The **tired** child was crabby.

present participle　　　　　　　　　　*past participle*

Circle each present or past participle. Draw an arrow to the noun it modifies. Write *pres* for present participle or *past* for past participle.

_____ Zelda's favorite book is the battered one on the middle shelf.

_____ You must stay away from the whirling power saw blade.

_____ We avoided the broken glass in the parking garage.

_____ The enraged hornet flew after the horse.

_____ Mike prefers to avoid the spinning rides.

_____ Polly, the parakeet, always bothers the napping puppy.

_____ The thawed desserts are in the refrigerator.

_____ Bailey will blow out the burning candles.

_____ Joel could not open the tightly closed jar.

_____ Earl washed the serving bowl and put it away.

_____ The reading area was full, so Sam read at his desk.

_____ Maddie put her muddied shoes on the deck.

🔍 Review Work

Underline the simple subjects once and the simple predicates twice.

✏️ Draft Book

Write 10 sentences that use present and past participles. Draw an arrow from each participle to the noun it modifies.

Name _____

▶ They're Confused

Usually, a regular verb forms the past tense and past participle by adding *d* or *ed* to the present tense verb. An irregular verb forms the past tense and past participle by changing spelling and can end with *t*, *en*, or *n*.

examples: bite ⟶ bitten   The robber was bitten by the police dog.
freeze ⟶ frozen   The frozen yogurt was delicious.

Circle the correct verbs and participles.

The mother blue jay has (sitted, sat) on her eggs for many days.

Her (shrinked, shrunken) shirt was never worn again.

The towering, old pine had (fell, fallen) during the snowstorm.

Abby will have (spoked, spoken) on the phone for two hours.

The girls had (swinged, swung) on the tire swing before us.

Ralph and Perry have (swimmed, swum) in Lake Michigan before.

The nanny goat at the zoo had (ate, eaten) the lace off my sock.

Tyrone had (setted, set) his camera on the picnic table.

The carefully (maked, made) wedding cake was beautiful.

The fishermen had (arosed, arisen) before the sun came up.

Cyndi has (catched, caught) several monarch butterflies in his net.

That nasty hornet had (stinged, stung) Sasha's hand.

Xena and Sean have (slided, slid) down the snowy hill on their sled.

The (broke, broken) vase laid in pieces on the floor.

 Review Work

Circle the plural nouns.

 Draft Book

Write 10 sentences using irregular verbs. Underline the verbs with blue. Underline the nouns with yellow.

Name _____

▶ Just to Be Perfect ⟩ perfect tenses

The three perfect verb tenses indicate completed action. They are formed using the past participle (usually verb + *d* or *ed*) and the helping verbs *had, has,* or *(will) have.*

past perfect: She **had known** the answer.
present perfect: She **has known** the answer.
future perfect: She **will have known** the answer.

Circle each past participle and its helping verb(s). Write *SP* for past perfect, *PP* for present perfect, or *FP* for future perfect on the line.

_____ Belinda has burned her tongue on that hot marshmallow.

_____ Val will have done her work.

_____ Lara will have dived off the high dive.

_____ Aubry and Kara have bitten into their apples.

_____ Fletcher will have biked to the video store.

_____ The sheep will have gone to the back pasture.

_____ Ella's cat has caught a mouse.

_____ The quarter has fallen into the drain.

_____ Aleta had worked on her science project.

_____ Gran had traveled to Alaska with Gramps.

_____ Darby and Kris will have spoken to Ms. Stallings.

_____ The small green snake has slithered into the grass.

_____ Flynn has asked for a large root beer float.

_____ The baby koala had clung to its mother's fur.

_____ Niki had taken her craft set home.

_____ The sun had shone all week long.

🔍 Review Work

Underline the complete subjects once.

✏️ Draft Book

Write 10 sentences using the perfect tense forms of verbs. Underline the verbs with blue.

▶ Ongoing Action ▷ progressive tense

The progressive verb tense indicates action in progress. It uses the present participle (verb + *ing*) and a form of the helping verb *to be*. Present progressive tense uses *am, is,* and *are*. Past progressive tense uses *was* and *were*. Future progressive tense uses *will be*.

Circle each progressive verb and its helping verb(s). Write *SPg* for past, *PPg* for present, or *FPg* for future on the line.

_____ The pot of spaghetti noodles was boiling for seven minutes.

_____ The crickets will be chirping all night long.

_____ Hal is sneezing.

_____ Abby was coughing all night.

_____ Melanie is swinging in the backyard.

_____ The ice-cream truck is coming up the street.

_____ The children will be swimming at the lake.

_____ The guinea pigs were playing hide-and-seek with the children.

_____ My sister Laine is knitting a sweater for my birthday.

_____ Jerome is working on the computer.

_____ Jolene was drinking a chocolate-caramel shake.

_____ Ian is biking to Jeremy's house.

_____ Grandma Judy was buying produce at the farmers' market.

_____ We will be visiting the museum on Tuesday.

_____ Nick is hammering the board into the joist.

🔍 Review Work

Circle the plural nouns.

✏️ Draft Book

Write 10 sentences using progressive tense verbs. Underline the verbs with blue.

▶ How, Where, or When ▷ adverbs

Adverbs are words that modify verbs, adjectives, or other adverbs. They tell how often, where, when, or to what extent something happens. Most adverbs end in *ly*. Three commonly used adverbs are *not*, *very*, and *too*.

Circle each adverb. Indicate how it modifies by writing *how*, *where*, *when*, or *what* on the line.

_____ Grace quickly finishes her paper.

_____ Addie always reminds us to buckle our seat belts.

_____ Rhonda and I ate a large breakfast this morning.

_____ The barking dog was annoyingly loud.

_____ The exhausted children went inside.

_____ Lane frequently drinks milk with his meals.

_____ The athlete gracefully executed the flip.

_____ Heath plays too much golf.

_____ Brenda silently crept up the stairs.

_____ Clare and Malory read often.

_____ Lisa chatters incessantly.

_____ Dad drove backward into the garage.

_____ Juan played the music quietly.

_____ Winnie will work on her painting tonight.

_____ The fruit salad is very healthy.

_____ The plan was brilliantly thought out.

_____ The storm wildly pounded the windows.

_____ Dean walks daily with his friend.

🔍 Review Work

Circle the adjectives. Draw and arrow from each adjective to the noun it describes.

✏️ Draft Book

Write a story about your favorite month of the year. Include adverbs. Circle the adverbs with purple.

Name _____

▶ Good or Well

Good, well, bad, and *badly* are often confused. *Good* and *bad* are adjectives. *Well* and *badly* are adverbs.

Circle the correct words. Draw an arrow from each adjective to the noun it describes.

The dancers performed the number (good, well).

Rita tried not to choose any (bad, badly) peaches.

Luke plans to rent a (good, well) video.

Arnie says he fishes (good, well) when he is in the boat.

Larry felt (bad, badly) when his bike was stolen.

Millicent did (good, well) on her last math test.

That story isn't written (bad, badly).

I can't hear (good, well) when the television is so loud.

Annabelle is not a (bad, badly) golfer.

Plug your ears because my sister sings (bad, badly).

Uma wants to do a (good, well) job on her sculpture.

They got lost because of the (bad, badly) set of directions.

That book is so (good, well), I would recommend it to anyone.

The chocolate cake with fudge icing is (good, well).

If Evan hits (bad, badly) in this game, he will probably practice all weekend.

We want a (good, well) baby-sitter; the last one was (bad, badly).

The play was (good, well), but the lead actor performed (bad, badly).

 Review Work

Draw an X next to each proper noun that names a person.

 Draft Book

Write 10 sentences. Include an adjective or adverb from this page in each sentence.

▶ Glasses and Sleep ▷ time adverbs

Adverbs modify verbs, adjectives, or other adverbs. Time adverbs tell when or how often. Time adverbs include: *before, continuously, early, eventually, finally, first, frequently, immediately, last night, lately, never, nightly, now, often, once, periodically, rarely, sometimes, soon, then, today, tonight, tomorrow,* and *usually.*

Write a time adverb on each line. Use words from the list above. Do not use words more than once.

Brett _____ loses his glasses.

They are _____ found in odd places.

His glasses were _____ found on the drinking fountain.

_____ , he left them on the ground next to the soccer field.

_____ , the dog found them and chewed them.

His mother is taking him to get new glasses _____ .

Brett promised _____ to leave his glasses lying around again.

Sylvia is _____ wide awake and attentive.

She is very tired _____ .

Sylvia did not get much sleep _____ .

Her baby brother cried _____ .

_____ , she drifted off to sleep.

We hope they both sleep better _____ .

Choose a time adverb not used in the sentences above. Use it in a sentence of your own.

_____

_____

🔍 **Review Work**

Underline the subject pronouns with red.

✏ **Draft Book**

Begin a list of time adverbs to use in future writing assignments. Write 10 sentences with adverbs.

Name _____

▶ Crawly Things

Adverbs can modify verbs, adjectives, or other adverbs, but they usually modify verbs. Place adverbs tell where.

Circle the place adverbs.

Many crawly things live outside.

I like them better there than inside.

They seem to be everywhere you look.

They are below, above, and beside.

Ants congregate underground.

Worms live there, too.

Mosquitoes seem to be anywhere people are.

One buzzed close to my ear.

Insects are always nearby.

Dragonflies hover overhead.

That apple has a worm inside.

Bluebirds swoop down to grab insects.

A chameleon looks backward for insects.

Paulina would like it if spiders lived far away.

A spider's web is over there.

An orb spider dropped down to wrap an insect for dinner.

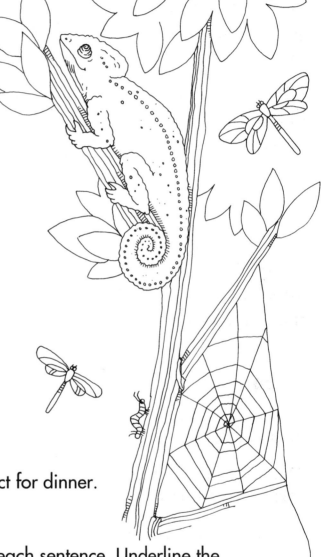

⌕ Review Work

Write an *SS* above the simple subject in each sentence. Underline the verbs with blue.

✎ Draft Book

Begin a list of place adverbs to use in future writing assignments. Write 10 sentences with adverbs.

Name _____

How'd You Do That? > manner adverbs

Adverbs can modify verbs, adjectives, or other adverbs, but they usually modify verbs. Manner adverbs tell how or in what manner an action is performed. Many end in *ly*.

Circle each manner adverb. Draw an arrow to the verb it modifies.

The kitten and puppy playfully ran from one end of the room to the other.

Jolene appeared calm but one foot tapped nervously.

Liza smiled confidently as she waved good-bye to her parents.

The children waited expectantly for the movie to begin.

Many fireworks exploded simultaneously in the night sky.

Louis likes to read aloud to the kindergartners.

Amber and I walked together to soccer practice.

We were completely surprised by the announcement.

Wilbur worked diligently to finish his project by Friday.

Quincy carefully climbed the maple tree to get the kitten down.

Ian quickly rode his bike home in order to meet his curfew.

Meg regretfully completed the exciting book.

Maddie intently watched the ants carry load after load into the anthill.

Janet maliciously tore Peter's artwork.

Pam immediately doused the paper fire with water.

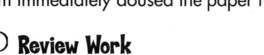

Review Work

Underline the nouns with yellow.

Draft Book

Begin a list of manner adverbs to use in future writing assignments. Write 10 sentences with adverbs.

Name _____

Comparatives

adverbs: positive, comparative, superlative

Adverbs describe and/or compare verbs, adjectives, and other adverbs. There are three degrees of comparison. The positive degree describes a verb, adjective, or other adverb. The comparative degree compares two actions (add *er* or the words *more* or *less*). The superlative degree compares more than two actions (add *est* or the words *most* or *least*).

If an adverb ends with *ly*, use *more*, *most*, *less*, or *least* in front of it: alertly (positive), more alertly (comparative), most alertly (superlative).

Add *er* and *est* to each adverb to make the comparative and superlative forms.

Positive: late, calm, near, soon, early

Comparative: _____

Superlative: _____

Add *more* and *most* to each adverb to make the comparative and superlative forms.

Positive: safely, skillfully, brilliantly, easily

Comparative: _____

Superlative: _____

Circle the comparative and superlative adverbs. Write which form of the adverb is used on each line.

_____   Delia answered more rapidly than Krysti.

_____   Ellie woke up the earliest.

_____   Simon returned home sooner than expected.

_____   I can finish this more quickly if you let me do it myself.

_____   Judy described the directions the most clearly.

_____   The youngest puppy most eagerly attacked the bone.

Review Work

Underline the simple predicate in each sentence with blue.

Draft Book

Write 10 sentences using comparative and superlative forms of adverbs.

▶ Fruits and Veggies

articles: a, an, the

A, *an*, and *the* are articles. An article comes before a noun or adjective/noun combination. Use *a* in front of words that start with a consonant sound. Use *an* in front of words that start with a vowel sound. Use *the* if reference is being made to a specific thing or things.

Write *a* or *an* in front of these items.

_____ apricot	_____ Macintosh apple	_____ tomato
_____ onion	_____ yam	_____ orange
_____ pear	_____ eggplant	_____ peach
_____ apple	_____ cantaloupe	_____ avocado
_____ honeydew	_____ artichoke	_____ Empire apple
_____ cherry	_____ watermelon	_____ banana

Write a, *an*, or *the* on each line.

I am making _____ salad. Would you help me? Bring me _____ lettuce

from _____ refrigerator. Please get _____ spinach and _____ endive

leaf. Cut _____ celery stalk and _____ cucumber into slices. You can slice

_____ onion, too. _____ radishes and _____ carrots are in the crisper.

_____ fruit salad would be good, also. There is _____ orange, _____

apple, and _____ banana on the counter. _____ cherries and _____

grapes are washed and in _____ bowl behind _____ milk. Put _____

sliced watermelon and _____ cubed cantaloupe on a plate. There is _____

honeydew on the shelf. It can be sliced and put on _____ plate.

🔍 Review Work

Underline the subject pronouns with red.

✏️ Draft Book

Find a story in your Draft Book. Circle the articles with orange. If an article is incorrect, fix it.

The Entire Thing — complete subject

The simple subject is the noun that the sentence is about. The complete subject is the simple subject plus any articles or adjectives that describe or modify that noun.

example: The striped ball rolled down the hill.
ball = simple subject
The striped ball = complete subject

article   adjective

Circle the simple subjects. Underline the complete subjects.

An itsy-bitsy bug will crawl under your beach towel.

Those five scary costumes were chosen for the play.

That incredibly high roller coaster causes people to scream.

The earsplitting tornado rampaged through town.

Those sharp knives have protective covers on them.

Our old, battered road atlas helped us determine travel routes.

Those neon-colored crayons add vibrant details to pictures.

My icy-cold fingers will need a pair of warm mittens.

Meg's little sister played the game all afternoon.

That very long number is not a palindrome.

Keith's sunburned shoulders hurt.

Irene Swanson moved to Arkansas.

That smelly lotion tingles on my skin.

The luminescent insects flickered on and off in the quiet darkness.

 Review Work

Underline the simple predicates with blue. Write the verb tense beside each sentence: S = past, P = present, and F = future.

 Draft Book

Write 10 sentences. Circle the simple subjects and underline the complete subjects.

Name _____

▶ Get the Rest ▶ complete predicate

The simple predicate is the verb that tells what someone or something is doing. The complete predicate is the simple predicate plus any helping or linking verbs and any adverbs that describe or modify the verb.

example: The marble can roll smoothly.
roll = simple predicate
can roll smoothly = complete predicate

helping verb   adverb

Circle the simple predicates. Underline the complete predicates.

The black and brown puppy may have been bought already.

That spotted dog often races around.

A hornet will sting quickly.

Little brown tree frogs buzz continuously.

The colorful parrot squawked most loudly.

The little golden hamster scurries around.

Mourning doves will wake up earliest.

The marble-sized hail suddenly pounded down.

The glowing coals shimmered more brightly.

Dolphins must surface often.

The number four race car accelerated rapidly.

Amber often works slowly but accurately.

That large stain will need prompt attention.

This disgusting tasting medicine was swallowed very quickly.

 ## Review Work

Indicate the verb tense used in each sentence. Write the verb tense beside each sentence: S = past, P = present, and F = future.

 ## Draft Book

Write 10 sentences with helping verbs and adverbs modifying the simple predicates. Underline the complete predicates with blue.

© Carson-Dellosa

▶ The Whole Predicate ▷ complete predicate

The complete predicate is the simple predicate plus any helping or linking verbs, any adverbs, and any other words that modify the verb. If the words are not part of the complete subject, they are included in the complete predicate.

example: Bob <u>will (bike) to the beach</u>.

The big, red apple <u>(fell) to the ground</u>.

Sally <u>(played) with her brother</u>.

Circle the simple predicates. Underline the complete predicates.

Violet was responsible for feeding the fish.

The glass of soda spilled across the table.

The sun sparkles blindingly off the snow.

The enormous block tower toppled.

Sleepy children awoke to frosted windows.

The winter snowman melted away to nothing.

Madalen slept with one arm around her teddy bear.

The price of stamps will rise at the end of June.

The glowing space heater pumps out waves of comforting heat.

The dinner-plate-sized blooms popped open overnight.

The striped beach ball drifted just out of reach.

Alicia surfaced coughing and sputtering.

This suction cup will stick securely to the window.

 Review Work

Indicate the verb tense used in each sentence. Write the verb tense beside each sentence: S = past, P = present, and F = future.

 Draft Book

Write 10 sentences. Underline the complete predicates with blue.

▶ Looking for Sentences ▶ complete sentences

A sentence needs one complete subject and one complete predicate.

example: <u>Jan</u> <u>has a dog</u>. = sentence

         ↑   ↑

complete subject   complete predicate

      a dog = not a sentence

A sentence can be long or short.

example: <u>Jan</u> <u>walks</u>.

       ↑   ↑

complete subject   complete predicate

    <u>The tiny little bird with the broken wing</u> ← *complete subject*
    <u>finally flew out the door and into the backyard</u>. ← *complete predicate*

If the group of words is a sentence, put a star in the box. Underline the complete subject once and the complete predicate twice. If the group of words is not a sentence, put an X in the box.

☐ Janelle, the girl with red hair	☐ Pamela likes to draw
☐ is a great talent	☐ a dollar or more
☐ Adelle took a peek at the bird's nest	☐ goodness, that room is messy
☐ a quadrilateral is a four-sided shape	☐ have a pet frog
☐ Larry handed in his assignment	☐ you can order a book

🔍 **Review Work**

Add an uppercase letter at the beginning and the correct punctuation mark at the end of each group of words that is a sentence.

✏️ **Draft Book**

Make complete sentences out of the groups of words that are not sentences.

Name _____

A sentence needs one complete subject and one complete predicate. A sentence fragment is a group of words missing either the subject or the predicate.

Add a subject or predicate to each sentence fragment to make a complete sentence. Put an uppercase letter at the beginning and the correct punctuation mark at the end.

wandering down the path through the woods

_____

Rosario, who arrived from South America,

_____

gathered the ingredients

_____

the animal in the very last cage

_____

the most incredible thing

_____

fell asleep on the couch

_____

ran across the sand

_____

are detailed and accurate

_____

stepped on its tail

_____

 Review Work

Underline the complete subjects once and the complete predicates twice.

 Draft Book

Choose one sentence from above and use it in a story.

Name _____

▶ Predicate Nouns

A linking verb does not show action. It links or joins something in the predicate to the subject of the sentence. It does not have an action verb after it. A predicate noun is a noun that follows the linking verb and tells something about the subject.

Underline the linking verbs. Circle the predicate nouns. Draw an arrow from each predicate noun to the simple subject it tells more about.

The zebra mussel is a bivalve originally from Europe.

That girl in the third row was my sister.

Mrs. Stamey is a fifth-grade teacher.

I am a good student.

A solar calculator is a great math tool.

Jupiter is a massive ball of gas.

Venus is the second planet from the sun.

The first-chair trombone player is Marcus Bolan.

Our sun is actually a star.

That lumpy, dark green stone is raw jade.

This blue, white, and green yarn will be an afghan someday.

Those ladies are the staff surgeons tonight.

That very large spider appears to be a tarantula.

Acrophobia is the fear of heights.

 ## Review Work

Circle the adverbs with purple.

 ## Draft Book

Write 10 sentences that use linking verbs and predicate nouns.
Draw an arrow from each predicate noun to the subject it tells more about.

Name _____

▶ Summertime

A linking verb does not show action. It links or joins something in the predicate to the subject of the sentence. It does not have an action verb after it. A predicate adjective is an adjective that follows the linking verb and tells something about the subject.

Underline the linking verbs. Circle the predicate adjectives. Draw an arrow from each predicate adjective to the simple subject it tells more about.

Ants in the house are disgusting.

Juicy hamburgers on the grill are delicious.

That backyard deck was unvarnished.

Jenna's batting abilities are poor.

The sunburn across my shoulders is painful.

The dent from the baseball was sizable.

Terrance will feel sick if he eats that whole bag of candy.

Luke's back was sore from shoveling sand into the sandbox.

Mrs. Tribble was enraged when she saw what those raccoons did to her garbage.

Wendy and I were unhappy with our performance on the tennis courts.

The twins were tired after swimming all afternoon.

Helping Mr. Green in the garden all day became boring.

The canoe trip was enjoyable.

That girl watching the otters is captivated by their antics.

That photograph is more breathtaking than your last one.

Grandmother was enchanted with the flowers we picked for her.

 Review Work

Write a D above each demonstrative adjective.

 Draft Book

Write 10 sentences that use linking verbs and predicate adjectives. Draw an arrow from each predicate adjective to the subject it tells more about.

▶ Take Your Pick ▷ predicate adjectives and nouns

Predicate adjectives and predicate nouns follow linking verbs. They tell something about the subject.

Underline the linking verbs. Circle each predicate adjective and each predicate noun. Write *PA* for predicate adjective or *PN* for predicate noun.

_____ Fireflies are fascinating insects.

_____ A galaxy is a group of stars and all the planets that surround them.

_____ Their cabin is cozy.

_____ Abigail is my lab partner.

_____ My jaw is hurting from chewing so much gum.

_____ The book is becoming more interesting.

_____ Your idea is creative.

_____ A driver is a golf club.

_____ That pumpkin is absolutely huge.

_____ Arya was thrilled to be voted class representative.

_____ Our puppy is excited to go for a walk.

_____ Numismatics is the hobby of coin collecting.

_____ Ian was happy to begin reading the new book.

🔍 Review Work

Draw an arrow from each predicate adjective or predicate noun to the simple subject it tells more about.

✏️ Draft Book

Write 10 sentences that use linking verbs and predicate adjectives or nouns. Draw an arrow from each predicate adjective or noun to the subject it tells more about.

▶ Explain It

appositives

An appositive is a word or phrase that explains, identifies, or gives information about another word. It comes after the word and usually is enclosed in a set of commas. At the end of a sentence, an appositive is enclosed by a comma and the ending punctuation.

example: My paper, **the one due tomorrow**, is done.

Circle each appositive. Draw an arrow to the noun it modifies.

Lake Superior, one of the Great Lakes, is the largest freshwater lake in the world.

Manatees, aquatic mammals, are very gentle creatures.

Jill and Willie watched the aurora borealis, the northern lights, shimmer across the sky.

Chambered nautiluses, living fossils, live in the Indian and South Pacific Oceans.

Speculation exists that water, a beverage needed for life, may be frozen on the moon.

Ludwig van Beethoven, a deaf musician, conducted the first performance of his Ninth Symphony.

Marie Curie, the only person to receive the Nobel Prize in both chemistry and physics, worked with radioactive materials.

Emma, the neighbor's dog, loves tomatoes.

Monarchs, migrating butterflies, winter in Mexico.

Spiders, members of the arachnid family, are not insects.

Valerie's family canoed around Thirty Thousand Islands, a coastal region on the Canadian side of Lake Huron.

Humberto works with an electron microscope, a device used to see minute objects.

 Review Work

Underline the complete subjects in the sentences. If the appositive modifies the simple subject, it is part of the complete subject.

 Draft Book

Write 10 sentences using appositives.

▶ It Was Done to Whom? ▷ direct objects

A direct object is the noun or pronoun that receives the action of the verb. It is located in the complete predicate. To locate the direct object, find the verb. Find a noun after the verb that answers *whom* or *what*. If a verb is acting on the noun, the noun is the direct object.

    example: The ball hit Tammi.
                 verb   *noun*

Tammi is the direct object because the ball hit or acted on her.

    example: I sent Chad some money.
            verb   *nouns*

Money is the direct object because the money was sent, not Chad.

Underline the verbs. Circle the direct objects.

The courtyard fountain continuously gushed water.

Leona frequently chews gum.

The anxious filly kicked the stall door.

Erica handed Jacob her paper.

Rochelle stowed the luggage in the overhead bin.

The heavy box squashed my foot.

Danielle offered her chocolate cupcake to Jesse.

The children broke the new vase.

Rosa canceled her subscription to the magazine.

Yolanda crochets a blue and white afghan.

The hot chicken soup burned April's tongue.

Enrique toasted a marshmallow over the campfire.

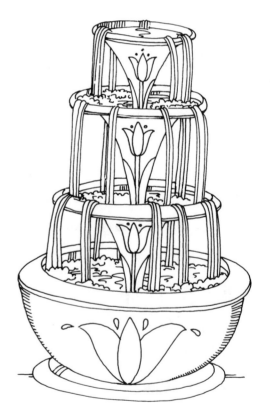

🔍 Review Work

    Underline the simple subjects with yellow.

✏️ Draft Book

    Write 10 sentences using direct objects. Circle each direct object.

Name _____

 # It Was Done for Whom?

indirect objects

An indirect object is the noun or pronoun that answers to whom or for whom (for what). It is located in the complete predicate and usually comes between the verb and the direct object.

example: Everet handed **Harry** a dollar.

verb   indirect object   direct object

Harry is the indirect object because the dollar was handed to him.

Underline the verbs once. Underline the direct objects twice. Circle the indirect objects.

José gave the struggling puppy a bath.

Peter wished his grandmother a happy birthday.

Walter gave Alan the tire swing.

The waiter handed Kent his burger platter.

Quinn, the girl who sits back there, offered Tommy her pencil.

Aunt May knitted June a new, yellow scarf.

Mr. Slider gave the chair a coat of varnish.

The first graders sent Santa lengthy letters in November.

The new neighbor made our family stir-fry.

Roberta saved Rico some sweet corn.

Franco sent his friends invitations to his pool party.

Allison served her family iced lemonade.

Lydia throws Stanton her beach towel.

Albert will save Jerome a seat on the bus after school.

Carlie lent Li her orange umbrella with the polished wood handle.

 ## Review Work

Write an *SS* above the simple subject in each sentence.

 ## Draft Book

Write 10 sentences using indirect objects. Circle the indirect object in each sentence.

Name _____

▶ Here They Are ⟩ prepositions

A preposition is a word or group of words that shows a relationship between two words in the sentence. It can tell where something is, where something is going, when something happens, or the relationship between a noun or pronoun and another word. Compound prepositions are multiple prepositions used together.

Single Prepositions Include:

aboard, about, above, across, after, against, along, alongside, among, around, as, at, before, behind, below, beneath, beside, besides, between, beyond, but, by, despite, down, during, except, for, from, in, inside, into, like, near, of, off, on, onto, out, outside, over, past, round, since, through, throughout, till, to, toward, under, underneath, until, up, upon, with, within, without

Compound Prepositions Include:

according to, ahead of, along with, as for, away from, because of, by way of, due to, except for, in addition to, in back of, in case of, in front of, in regard to, in spite of, instead of, out of, up to, with the exception of

Write three sentences using single prepositions and three sentences using compound prepositions.

_____

_____

_____

_____

_____

_____

🔍 Review Work

Circle the prepositions in the sentences. Underline the nouns with yellow and the verbs with blue.

✏️ Draft Book

Choose 10 prepositions from the lists above and write unique phrases, such as "aboard our flying saucer one night." Use these phrases as creative story starters.

▶ Identifying Prepositions ▶ prepositional phrases

A preposition is a word or group of words that shows a relationship between two words in the sentence. It can tell where something is, where something is going, when something happens, or the relationship between a noun or pronoun and another word. Compound prepositions are multiple prepositions used together.

A prepositional phrase begins with a preposition and ends with a noun or pronoun. The noun or pronoun in a prepositional phrase is called the object of the preposition. A preposition always has an object. If the word does not have an object, it is not acting as a preposition. A sentence can have more than one prepositional phrase.

example: The book **on the desk** is mine.

preposition   *object*

Box the prepositions. Circle the objects of the prepositions. Underline the prepositional phrases.

The Arabian mare thundered around the corral.

Ellen's sunset photograph is hanging on our living room wall.

Kaela ordered a thick milkshake instead of an ice-cream cone.

Jena hugged her horse with all her strength.

Gina walked carefully around the edge of the pond.

The washed grapes are in the blue bowl.

Maddie slept with her thumb in her mouth.

Mr. Tennison has a bag of jelly beans in his desk drawer.

The box of books is located behind the door.

The jar of homemade strawberry jam did not last long.

We are renting the cottage near the dock.

Blaine wiped up the spill with a paper towel.

 Review Work

Write an *SS* above the simple subject in each sentence.

 Draft Book

Write 10 sentences using prepositional phrases. Underline the prepositions.

▶ Tell About Nouns ▷ adjective prepositional phrases

Prepositional phrases show relationships. Prepositional phrases can modify nouns or verbs. An adjective prepositional phrase shows a relationship between a noun and the object of the preposition. It modifies a noun or pronoun just like a one-word adjective.

example: Hubert ate a huge piece (of blueberry pie).

noun adjective prepositional phrase

Circle each adjective prepositional phrase. Draw an arrow to the noun or pronoun it modifies.

The candle on the piano is vanilla scented.

Use that container of fertilizer to feed the plants.

The books from the library must be returned today.

Anna likes pancakes with butter and maple syrup.

That radish in the salad is very spicy.

The boy near the slide helped me pick up trash.

The horse with the green saddle blanket won the prize.

Students throughout the school want a longer lunch period.

The girl with chicken pox ate lunch with my sister yesterday.

Julie ordered marble cake with Bavarian cream filling and chocolate frosting.

Esai shoveled the end of the driveway.

The red scarf around my neck was knitted by Pam.

Our class will clean up the mess around the ball field.

🔍 Review Work

Underline the object of the preposition in each sentence.

✏️ Draft Book

Write 10 sentences using adjective prepositional phrases. Underline each preposition and draw an arrow to the noun or pronoun it modifies.

Name _____

▶ Which Verb? ▶ adjective prepositional phrases and noun-verb agreement

When an adjective prepositional phrase modifies the simple subject, the subject (not the object of the preposition) must agree with the verb.

example: A can of peaches falls on the floor. (yes)
A can of peaches fall on the floor. (no)
The verb must agree with the simple subject *can.*

Underline the simple subjects once. Underline the prepositional phrases twice. Circle the correct verbs.

The buttons on her sweater (is, are) wooden.

The dog with many spots (growl, growls) at anyone entering that yard.

The people throughout the area (want, wants) this road to have a four-way stop.

The girl with braces (brushes, brush) her teeth twice a day.

The parking places outside the mall (need, needs) plowing.

The couch with green and brown stripes (is, are) comfortable.

A bucket of blueberries (cost, costs) four dollars.

That pack of pencils (is, are) inexpensive.

The sweaters in that display (fit, fits) me.

Many marbles in that game (are, is) matching.

The pictures of the zoo trip (are, is) developed.

Many socks in her drawer (do, does) not match.

The guinea pig with black spots (need, needs) a good home.

The videos on the bottom shelf (need, needs) to be returned.

That banana with many dark spots (is, are) destined for banana bread.

 Review Work

Draw a box around the object of each preposition.

 Draft Book

Write 10 sentences using adjective prepositional phrases. Make the simple subjects and verbs agree.

Name _____

Tell About Verbs
adverb prepositional phrases

Prepositional phrases show relationships. Prepositional phrases can modify nouns or verbs. An adverb prepositional phrase modifies the verb. It tells how, where, when, or to what extent something happens just like a one-word adverb.

Underline each adverb prepositional phrase. Tell how it modifies the verb by writing *how*, *where*, *when*, or *what* on the line.

_____ The trip photos are in the album.

_____ David and Walter walked to the store.

_____ The pitcher played beyond his average performance.

_____ During yesterday's thunderstorm, the power went out.

_____ The Girl Scout troop will sleep at Ms. Emma's house Friday night.

_____ Without any complaining, Jade cleaned her room.

_____ Olivia must be home before 7:00 p.m.

_____ Geno will put that can into the recycle bin.

_____ Their family vacations in June.

_____ My dad ate ice cream and cookies until he was full.

_____ Ned and I finished the project with assistance.

_____ He went straight to his room.

_____ Shelly found many monarch caterpillars on the milkweed plants.

_____ We will visit our cousins over the holiday break.

_____ On Saturday night, we saw the northern lights.

_____ The neighborhood children had a snowball battle despite the freezing temperatures.

Review Work

Underline the simple subjects with yellow.

Draft Book

Write 10 sentences using a variety of adverb prepositional phrases.

▶ The Difference ▶ adverb or adverb prepositional phrases

Many of the same words can be used as adverbs or to begin adverb prepositional phrases. A prepositional phrase always has an object of the preposition.

adverb: The dog ran **around**.

preposition: The dog ran **around** <u>the house.</u>

Identify each word in bold type. Write adverb or preposition.

_____ The beaver swam **to** his underwater door.

_____ Alejandro always flosses **between** his teeth.

_____ The coals are hot; you can put your hot dog **in**.

_____ The sails billowed **during** the boat ride.

_____ The bear crawled **in** his den and went to sleep.

_____ Dan sat **nearby** as the air show continued.

_____ Dolphins live **underneath** the ocean.

_____ When the rain started, we went **inside**.

_____ The crowd clapped as the band passed **by**.

_____ My little sister leaned **against** my leg while we were reading.

_____ Do not put the napkin on the plate; put it **underneath**.

_____ Rich and Lianne walked **along** the edge of the dune.

_____ The snow came **down** and covered the ground.

ρ Review Work

Underline the prepositional phrases. Circle the object of each preposition.

✎ Draft Book

Write 10 sentences using adverbs and adverb prepositional phrases.

A Group of Words
adverb or adverb prepositional phrases

Many of the same words can be used as adverbs or to begin adverb prepositional phrases. A prepositional phrase always has an object of the preposition.

adverb: The ship sank **below**.

preposition: The ship sank **below** the ocean.

Box each adverb and preposition. Underline each prepositional phrase.

Fred made the mixture for his cow.

They can leave for the park whenever.

The power has been out since Monday.

At three o'clock, we will go outside.

They are not moving until tomorrow.

Natasha recited her poem for the class.

We finished the papers before.

He came inside for a snack.

Willie set the rake against the garage.

A bluebird nest is in the tree.

We will stop for ice cream after the program.

 Review Work

Draw an arrow from each adverb or adverb prepositional phrase to the verb it modifies.

 Draft Book

Write 10 sentences using prepositions as adverbs and as adverb prepositional phrases. Identify how the preposition is used in each sentence: ADV = adverb and AP = adverb prepositional phrase.

Name _____

▶ Which Is Which? ▶ adjective and adverb prepositional phrases

Prepositional phrases show relationships. Prepositional phrases can modify nouns or verbs. An adjective prepositional phrase modifies the noun. An adverb prepositional phrase modifies the verb.

Underline the prepositional phrases. Write *Adj* above each adjective prepositional phrase and *Adv* above each adverb prepositional phrase.

Dion put the night crawlers into the bucket.

The bread in that bag is stale.

The beekeeper delivered his bees to the fruit orchard.

Talia reads a book in the morning.

The cow from that farm is standing in the middle of the road.

The Milky Way is only one of many galaxies in the universe.

The crystal clips held her hair off her forehead.

The box of chocolates melted in the trunk of the hot car.

Zach delivered the jar of homemade apricot jam.

On Monday morning, Irma jogged five miles.

Our team won the match despite playing on their field.

Amber walked through the door of the gym.

Make a turn off this road at the next stop sign.

Renee swam across the pool to the deep end.

 Review Work

Underline the verbs with blue.

 Draft Book

Write 10 sentences using prepositional phrases. Write *Adj* above each adjective prepositional phrase and *Adv* above each adverb prepositional phrase.

Name _____

▶ We Sound the Same ⟩ homophones

Homophones are words that sound alike but are spelled differently and have different meanings.

Write the correct homophone on each line.

its: possessive pronoun   **it's:** contraction for it is

_____ too late to go to the movie now.

The cottage has _____ own beach access.

_____ top is scratched.

Erica believes _____ too icy to drive to the library.

there: location word   **their:** possessive pronoun   **they're:** contraction for they are

_____ house is on the cul-de-sac at the end of the street.

_____ lots of fun to play games with.

Marcus and Cody went _____ for a cookout.

Riley really likes _____ llamas.

At the ice-cream shop, _____ having a two-for-one special today.

Tamika will rest _____ before biking the last six miles.

your: possessive pronoun   **you're:** contraction for you are

_____ visiting the zoo with us this Wednesday.

Do you like _____ new hot tub?

I'm sorry _____ not able to come to the cookout.

whose: interrogative pronoun   **who's:** contraction for who is

_____ were you planning to paint first?

There is no name on this paper; _____ is it?

The store wants to hire the student _____ the most reliable.

🔍 Review Work

Underline the nouns with yellow.

✏️ Draft Book

Write three sentences for each homophone on this page.

LC1.5

Name _____

An interrogative sentence asks a question. It ends with a question mark.

Write interrogative sentences that would be answered by each of the following statements. Put an uppercase letter at the beginning and a question mark at the end of each.

interrogative sentence: _____

It is on Friday.

interrogative sentence: _____

They are over there.

interrogative sentence: _____

It is over six feet tall.

interrogative sentence: _____

It must have been him.

interrogative sentence: _____

It is hers.

interrogative sentence: _____

It is in the United States.

interrogative sentence: _____

They live in the rain forest.

interrogative sentence: _____

It is less than three pounds.

Review Work

Underline the pronouns in the sentences with red.

Draft Book

Write 10 interrogative sentences and answers. Include pronouns in your answers.

▶ Science Class ▶ interrogative and declarative sentences

An interrogative sentence asks a question and ends with a question mark. A declarative sentence tells something and ends with a period.

Put the correct punctuation mark at the end of each sentence.

matter is anything that has mass and takes up space ☐

solids, liquids, and gases are the three states of matter ☐

did you that know solids and liquids can combine to produce a gas ☐

we put baking soda, a solid, into an empty aquarium ☐

we also put in five candles at varying heights ☐

then, we added vinegar, a liquid ☐

can you predict what happened ☐

the baking soda and vinegar combined in a chemical
reaction making carbon dioxide, a gas ☐

the evidence was the candles ☐

beginning with the shortest candle, the candles went out, one by one ☐

mrs. ames used a bubble wand to blow bubbles into the aquarium ☐

do you know what happened ☐

the bubbles floated right where the carbon dioxide and room air met ☐

carbon dioxide is heavier than room air ☐

the candles and bubbles showed where the layer of carbon dioxide ended ☐

🔍 Review Work

Review sentences for words that should start with uppercase letters. Cross out the lowercase letters and write the uppercase letters above them.

✏️ Draft Book

Write six interrogative and six declarative sentences. End each sentence with the correct punctuation mark.

 **Wow!** exclamatory sentences

An exclamatory sentence shows strong feelings and ends with an exclamation mark.

Rewrite each exclamatory sentence. Put uppercase letters where they belong and exclamation marks at the ends.

i passed the science test

_____

we got an invitation to the party

_____

the moon looks incredible tonight

_____

hey, don't step on my books

_____

this ice cream is fantastic

_____

don't throw my homework away

_____

jade won the contest

_____

 Review Work

Choose one sentence from above and draw a star next to it. If that sentence is the answer, what is the question?

_____

Draft Book

Write 10 exclamatory sentences. End each sentence with an exclamation mark.

Name _____

▶ With Feeling ▷ imperative sentences

A sentence that tells you what to do or gives you a command is called an imperative sentence. Most imperative sentences end with periods. Occasionally, a command is given with great feeling. In this case, an exclamation mark is used. The same command can end with either a period or an exclamation mark depending on the situation.

example: Sit down. ⟶ Mom is asking you to sit down to dinner.
Sit down! ⟶ A small child is standing on a rocking chair, and it is about to tip over.

Read the situations. Put the correct punctuation at the end of each imperative sentence.

Stop that ☐ A friend is tapping her pencil.

Stop that ☐ Your brother is hitting your bruised shoulder.

Wash your hands ☐ Someone touched poison ivy.

Wash your hands ☐ It is dinnertime.

Put water on it ☐ A fire started in the trash can.

Put water on it ☐ The soil in the plant is beginning to dry.

Move ☐ Your friend is lounging on the couch, and you would like to share.

Move ☐ The bull has spotted your friend in his pasture and is racing toward her.

Get your dad ☐ It is time for dinner.

Get your dad ☐ The ladder fell down, and Mom is stuck on the roof.

🔍 Review Work

Give the situations for these two imperative sentences.

Run! _____

Run. _____

✏️ Draft Book

Write 10 imperative sentences. Begin each with an uppercase letter. End some sentences with periods and some with exclamation marks. Describe each situation.

Name _____

 # You, You, You

A sentence that tells you what to do or gives you a command is called an imperative sentence. Most imperative sentences end with a period. An imperative sentence looks like a complete predicate. The complete subject is *you*. *You* is implied, which means that since the speaker is talking to you, it is understood that *you* is the subject, even though the word *you* isn't always written.

Underline the complete predicates. Circle the simple predicates.

Brush your teeth after every meal.

Turn off the television so you can get ready for bed.

Call me as soon as you arrive.

Don't bring food into your bedroom.

Put the return address in the upper, left corner of the envelope.

Drink plenty of water so you won't get dehydrated.

Change the interrogative sentences to imperative sentences.

Will you pass the salt and pepper?

_____

Can you write Audrey a thank-you note this afternoon?

_____

Will you read the book and turn in a report by Monday?

_____

 Review Work

Change one imperative sentence from the top of the page to an interrogative sentence.

_____

 Draft Book

Write 10 imperative sentences. End each sentence with a period.

▶ New Pool

sentence types

There are four main types of sentences. A declarative sentence tells something and ends with a period. An interrogative sentence asks a question and ends with a question mark. An exclamatory sentence shows strong feelings and ends with an exclamation mark. An imperative sentence is a command. The subject *you* is implied. It usually ends in a period, but can end in an exclamation mark.

Write *declarative*, *interrogative*, *exclamatory*, or *imperative* on each line.

_____ We have the plans for putting a pool in our backyard.

_____ Would you like to see them?

_____ Don't touch the plans with dirty hands, please.

_____ Look right here.

_____ Can you see this area?

_____ It is the deep end.

_____ It's huge!

_____ They will begin to dig the hole for the pool next week.

_____ It will take three weeks until it is finished.

_____ Put your finger on the large area here.

_____ That whole area will be the deck.

_____ Did you know that we will have to build a fence, too?

_____ It has to be five feet tall for safety reasons.

_____ I can hardly wait!

🔍 Review Work

Underline the complete subjects once and the complete predicates twice.

✏️ Draft Book

Write four declarative, four interrogative, four exclamatory, and four imperative sentences. End each sentence with the correct punctuation mark.

► To + Verb

infinitives

Infinitives are present tense verbs that are usually preceded by the word *to*. An infinitive can act as a noun, adjective, or adverb.

Circle the infinitives.

We need to water the plants.

To be outstanding was Maria's goal.

To open the jar takes muscles.

You will need to remove the plastic liner.

Courage is needed to enter the haunted mansion.

To grill outside is best.

We want to enjoy the movie without a lot of extra noise.

Everyone would like to drink from the colder drinking fountain.

Abby and Pearl want to show the class how to make pancakes.

We will be ready to leave when all of the toys are picked up.

The buds on the yellow flowers are beginning to open.

Dad has to run to the store for more nails.

We have to clean up this mess.

Salando can't wait to go on vacation in December.

The baby began to crawl on the floor.

We must wait until this afternoon to swim in the pool.

You need five tokens to play the arcade games.

Daily teeth brushing helps to keep plaque from forming cavities.

Cleo wants to have that candy bar.

Regular practice is needed to excel at basketball.

Review Work

Write an *SS* above the simple subject in each sentence.

 ## Draft Book

Write 10 sentences using infinitives. Underline the infinitives.

Name _____

▶ He or Him?

Pronouns take the place of nouns. Subject pronouns take the place of subject nouns. Object pronouns take the place of nouns used as objects and are found in the complete predicate. Possessive pronouns take the place of possessive nouns. The possessive pronoun *its* does not have an apostrophe.

subject pronouns: I, you, he, she, we, they, it
object pronouns: me, you, her, him, them, us, it
possessive pronouns:
  before a noun: my, your, his, her, its, our, their
  after a linking verb: mine, yours, his, hers, its, ours, theirs

Circle the correct pronouns.

Sara and Bonnie took (they, them) to the matinee.

After the snowstorm, (us, we) helped shovel the walkway.

Cameron helped (she, her) find the lens to (her, hers) glasses.

(I, me) planted many seeds in (our, ours) garden.

Will (you, your) come with (I, me) to (their, theirs) house?

Joe loaned (he, his) new, leather baseball glove to (she, her).

Did (her, she) blame (we, us) for the broken window?

Tye will help Justin and (I, me) look for (it, its).

(We, Us) can build (it, its) over there in (your, yours) big tree.

Owen and (I, me) took an art course this summer.

(I, me) went with (he, him) to the library.

(They, Them) promised to come with (we, us) to the arcade across town.

The elephant tossed water on (their, theirs) clothing and mud on (our, ours).

Anna, (she, you) have (your, yours) own markers; quit borrowing (my, mine).

🔍 Review Work

Underline the prepositional phrases in the sentences.

✏️ Draft Book

Find a page of writing in your Draft Book and search for pronouns. Underline them with red. Make corrections where necessary.

Name _____

▶ This Is It

Pronouns take the place of nouns. The four demonstrative pronouns are the same as the four demonstrative adjectives: *this*, *that*, *these*, and *those*. A demonstrative pronoun takes the place of the noun rather than describes it.

singular (located nearby):   this   singular (located a distance away):   that
plural (located nearby):   these   plural (located a distance away):   those

Circle the demonstrative pronouns.

This will do a better job cleaning the windows than that.

These will taste better on the salad.

When it is snowing, those are the better boots to wear.

On your nose, that is the sunscreen to use.

When did those become fashionable?

In gym class, that is the most exciting game to play.

Those belong to Rasheed; put them in his desk.

During summer break, that is the place to meet people.

Those are her best recipes.

Circle the demonstrative words. Write *DP* for demonstrative pronoun or *DA* for demonstrative adjective above each word.

This is the watch belonging in that display case.

That is the best rake to use when those leaves fall.

This must be added to it before there is enough hose to water that area of the garden.

That is not the correct method to use when solving this problem.

Those are the people that obnoxious child came with.

This summer we will use that when picking those blueberries.

 **Review Work**

Underline other pronouns in the sentences with red.

 Draft Book

Write 10 sentences using demonstrative pronouns. Write *DP* above each demonstrative pronoun.

Name _____

▶ Someone Can

Pronouns take the place of nouns. Indefinite pronouns refer to nouns in a general way. Indefinite pronouns include the following words: *all, another, any, anybody, anyone, anything, both, each, either, everybody, everyone, everything, few, little, many, more, most, much, neither, nobody, none, no one, nothing, one, ones, other, others, several, some, somebody, someone,* and *something.*

Circle the indefinite pronouns.

Many will come to the museum this summer.

One came to the feeder this morning, and another came last night.

A few excited ones got the crowd going.

Only a few registered, but several arrived on the first day of camp.

I think somebody should clean up the marbles and game pieces.

Walter and Mason are at the door; either can mow the yard.

If someone gets home before me, he can put dinner in the oven.

Fruits and vegetables are delicious; each is good for a healthy, growing body.

Any who enter may choose their routes.

Jessie really wanted both of them.

No one chose to help with the clean-up activities.

Some have blue tags and others have red tags.

Nothing can be done about the misplaced invitation.

All of the leaves will fall from the tree at the end of summer.

Anyone can come to the amusement park if he is accompanied by an adult.

Several swam downstream into the lake.

 Review Work

Underline the prepositional phrases.

 Draft Book

Write 10 sentences using indefinite pronouns. Underline them with red.

Name _____

▶ I Myself

An intensive pronoun draws attention to or intensifies a noun or a pronoun. The intensive pronouns are:

singular: myself, yourself, himself, herself, itself
plural: ourselves, yourselves, themselves

These pronouns can also be reflexive pronouns. A reflexive pronoun "reflects" back to the subject of a sentence.

examples: intensive pronoun: Mr. Grump **himself** carved the cake.
reflexive pronoun: Ellie helped **herself** to the cake.

Circle the intensive and reflexive pronouns in the sentences below. Write *IP* for intensive pronoun or *RP* for reflexive pronoun on each line.

_____ Ned told himself it had to be a huge mistake.

_____ Delpha baked the brownies and made the punch herself.

_____ Pamela and Andrew introduced themselves to the new teacher.

_____ I timed myself to see how long it would take to walk to school.

_____ Last night, Maya and I completed the puzzle ourselves.

_____ The winner, Arthur himself, donated fifty books.

_____ Sally reminded herself that she had to be home by six o'clock.

_____ The bees themselves saved the farmer from loss.

_____ Emilie and I helped ourselves to that chocolate marshmallow ice cream.

_____ The ants helped themselves to some of our picnic.

_____ I myself took that piece of pizza.

_____ That class themselves sold over one thousand candy bars.

_____ The Baltimore oriole helped itself to birdseed and the sliced orange.

🔍 Review Work

Underline the simple subjects once and the simple predicates twice.

✏ Draft Book

Write 10 sentences using a variety of intensive and reflexive pronouns.

Name _____

▶ To or With Whom

Interrogative pronouns are used to ask questions. Sometimes they begin interrogative sentences. The five interrogative pronouns are: *what, which, who, whom,* and *whose. Who* is used like a subject pronoun; *whom* is used like an object pronoun. If these words are not being used in place of nouns, they are not interrogative pronouns.

Circle the interrogative pronouns in the sentences below.

I need to know which will fit you.

Which did you buy, the yellow or green one?

Big Store has what you need to finish the tree house.

The teacher knows with whom each person is working.

Whose are those platters of sandwiches?

What are they bringing to the holiday picnic?

The class planned with whom each student would read.

Mom wants to know who put her finger into the cake's frosting.

Whose should we enter in the city competition?

Who was talking before?

To whom were you speaking on the phone?

With whom do you plan to ride home?

We don't know whose those are.

Hal knows which has won the contest.

Janice knows which will produce the largest blooms.

Cindy doesn't know who will take her ticket.

Which did Andy choose as his puppy?

 **Review Work**

Change one declarative sentence from the top of the page to an interrogative sentence.

_____

 Draft Book

Write 10 sentences using interrogative pronouns.

Name _____

▶ Past the Verb ▶ object pronouns

An object pronoun takes the place of a noun found in the complete predicate. It can replace the direct object, indirect object, or object of the preposition. Object pronouns are: *me, you, her, him, them, us,* and *it.*

Replace each word in bold type with an object pronoun. Write the correct pronoun on the line.

Rebecca wanted **the new green ruler** to bring to school. _____

Amber gave **Mrs. Evans** the envelope with her lunch money. _____

Dawn sprayed the hose at **Jerry and Alicia**. _____

Mrs. Caron brought **Alexis and me** to the soccer field. _____

The dog chewed **Aunt Jackie's new green rug**. _____

The shoes with red laces were bought by **Chuck and Barry**. _____

Bobbi and Charlene gave **the miniature goat** some food pellets. _____

Marcus pushed **Justine** on the swings. _____

Vito bought ice cream bars for **Mike and me**. _____

Shupei skated at the rink with **Peter**. _____

Gerard, get onto **the sled** so we can go downhill. _____

A new family just moved in across from **Ariel**. _____

Use the object pronouns *me* and *you* to write two sentences below. Remember to place each object pronoun in the complete predicate.

> **example:** The bright sun gave me a headache.

_____

_____

 ## Review Work

Write *DO* for direct object, *IO* for indirect object, or *OP* for object of the preposition above each word in bold type in the sentences.

 ## Draft Book

Write a story about a picnic in the park using object pronouns. Underline the pronouns with red.

Name _____

▶ It Must Be Mine

Possessive pronouns take the place of possessive nouns. They can be used before a noun or after a linking verb. The possessive pronoun *its* does not have an apostrophe.

  before a noun: my, your, his, her, its, our, their

  after a linking verb: mine, yours, his, hers, its, ours, theirs

  example: **My** brush is on the table.   That brush is **mine**.

Circle each possessive pronoun. Draw an arrow to the noun it modifies.

Their mom travels around the state on business.

Our house is near the library.

Its handle is loose.

The black dog under that bush is mine.

Her socks are in the middle drawer.

We went to the musical with his parents.

The house with the pool is his.

My friend asked my opinion about which bike to buy.

The salami and cheese sandwich is hers.

Their wooded backyard is a great place to play.

Her older cousin is staying at their house for a week.

The trophy has its own shelf.

His old bunk bed was given to his younger brother.

 Review Work

  Underline the complete subjects in the sentences. If the possessive noun modifies the simple subject, it is part of the complete subject.

 Draft Book

  Write sentences using the list of possessive pronouns on this page. Use each possessive pronoun at least once.

Name _____

▶ Throw Some Out ▶ contractions

A contraction is two words that are put together to form one word. An apostrophe replaces the missing letters. Many contractions are formed using pronouns and other words. The following letters are left with the apostrophe when a contraction is made.

'll when adding *will* (that**'ll**)
'd when adding *would* or *had* (we**'d**)
's when adding *is* or *has* (she**'s**)
're when adding *are* (we**'re**)
've when adding *have* (I**'ve**)

Write the contractions.

I + would = _____   he + will = _____

it + is = _____   what + is = _____

they + would = _____   they + will = _____

Write the words that form the contractions.

he'd = _____   I'll = _____

there've = _____   I'm = _____

we'd = _____   she'll = _____

Circle each contraction. Write the words it replaces on the line.

_____ Do you think they've gone to the game without us?

_____ Kris and Jorge think they're not invited to the party.

_____ Willa said she'd bring a blanket to the camp out.

_____ Has Mrs. Holt decided who's making the announcement today?

_____ There's enough time to finish the card.

_____ I think I'll put the new video on the top shelf.

_____ Here's the key we looked for all morning!

🔍 Review Work

Underline the nouns with yellow.

✏️ Draft Book

Write a sentence using each contraction from this page.

Name _____

▶ Did Not!

A contraction is two words that are put together to form one word. An apostrophe replaces the missing letters. *Not* is a word that forms contractions with many helping or linking verbs. In contractions, the *o* in *not* is replaced with an apostrophe.

    example: did + not = didn't

The contraction for *will not* is an exception: will + not = won't.

Circle each contraction. Write the two words that formed it on the line.

_____ We aren't planning to attend the football game tonight.

_____ The plan itself isn't to sit around and do nothing.

_____ Rebecca wasn't in the band room this morning.

_____ Lara shouldn't have to do that by herself.

_____ The children mustn't put their dirty hands on the sliding door.

_____ That table can't take the load of all those bricks.

_____ Jeffrey hadn't done his homework.

_____ Alejandro wouldn't take a snack without asking.

_____ Kyra, Gabby, and Emma weren't at the park yesterday.

_____ The mail carrier hasn't driven down Maple Street yet.

_____ Mika, our new puppy, didn't want to sleep.

_____ Arabella and I haven't done our morning chores.

_____ Jon doesn't want to eat pizza.

_____ Many won't arrive until after the food booth opens.

_____ Ollie didn't have anyone to help him.

_____ The squirrels couldn't get onto the new bird feeder.

 Review Work

Underline each pronoun with red.

 Draft Book

Write a sentence using each contraction from this page.

Name _____

 **Combining Sentences** coordinating conjunctions

Sentences can be combined when their ideas are the same. Related sentences can be joined with coordinating conjunctions. There are seven coordinating conjunctions: *and, nor, but, for, yet, so,* and *or.*

examples: Alex plays tennis. + Alex plays basketball. =
Alex plays tennis and basketball.
Anika slept on the plane. + Anika did not sleep on the train. =
Anika slept on the plane but not on the train.

Combine each set of sentences using a coordinating conjunction. Write the new sentence on the line.

Devin went swimming in the pool. Devin did not go swimming in the lake.

_____

The flowers need to be watered. The flowers need to be fertilized.

_____

Joie remembered her backpack. Joie did not remember her lunch.

_____

We can watch the movie. We can play a game.

_____

I did not buy candy. I didn't buy chips.

_____

The squirrel jumped on the bird feeder. The squirrel ate the birdseed.

_____

Lekita likes broccoli. Lekita likes cauliflower.

_____

 Review Work

Circle the coordinating conjunctions.

 Draft Book

Write five pairs of sentences that can be combined. Write a combined sentence for each pair.

Name _____

Similar sentences can be combined into one simple sentence with a compound subject by using a coordinating conjunction.

example: Dan skated today. + Jack skated today. = Dan and Jack skated today.

Dan skated today. + Jack did not skate today. =
Dan but not Jack skated today.

If three or more subjects are combined, use commas to separate them and the conjunction.

example: Dan skated today. + Jack skated today. + Mark skated today. =
Dan, Jack, and Mark skated today.

Underline the compound subject in each sentence.

Blues, minkes, and sperm whales are known as great whales.

The biographies but not the anthologies are on the first shelf.

Joe, Max, Hilary, and Hope play trumpets in the band.

Andy and I bought ice-cream sandwiches.

Blue jays, finches, cardinals, and chickadees come daily to the bird feeder.

Use a coordinating conjunction to combine each set of sentences into one sentence with a compound subject. Write each sentence on a line.

Julissa ate salad. Elia ate salad.

_____

Jacob planted the corn. Jerez planted the corn.

_____

Dolphins are mammals. Whales are mammals. Manatees are mammals.

_____

 Review Work

In the combined sentences you wrote, underline the complete subjects once and the complete predicates twice.

 Draft Book

Write five sets of sentences containing first nouns that can be combined. Trade with a partner and combine the sentences.

Name _____

Doing Many Things

combining predicates

Similar sentences can be combined into one simple sentence with a compound predicate by using a coordinating conjunction.

example: Jon planted the seeds. + Jon watered the seeds. =
Jon planted and watered the seeds.

Underline the compound predicate in each sentence. Circle each coordinating conjunction.

The rocket ignited and blasted off into space.

Bradley and Ida washed, vacuumed, and waxed the car.

The dog broke the leash and ran away.

The wind whipped the tree's branches and shredded its leaves.

Egan catches and throws during practice.

Ellie whipped and folded the eggs into the batter.

Use a coordinating conjunction to combine each set of sentences into one sentence with a compound predicate. Write each sentence on a line.

William measured the board. William cut the board.

_____

Dianne swept the floor. Dianne mopped the floor. Dianne waxed the floor.

_____

The kitten pounced on the ball of yarn. The kitten swatted the ball of yarn.

_____

Pierre screamed on the roller coaster. Pierre enjoyed the roller coaster.

_____

 Review Work

In the combined sentences you wrote, underline the simple subjects once and the simple predicates twice.

 Draft Book

Write five sets of sentences whose verbs can be combined. Write a combined sentence for each set.

▶ We Can Relate ▶ compound subjects and predicates

Sentences can be combined when their ideas are the same. Related sentences can be joined with coordinating conjunctions.

Circle the coordinating conjunctions. If a sentence has a compound subject write CS. If a sentence has a compound predicate write CP. If it has both, write B.

_____ Salmon and walleye swim upstream in that river.

_____ Billy and Sara formed and threw snowballs.

_____ Bats and dragonflies eat mosquitoes.

_____ Taylor bought cotton candy and ate it.

_____ The grapes and apples fell and rolled on the floor.

_____ Prince and Buster growled at the intruder.

_____ The horseflies and mosquitoes irritated and pestered the hikers.

_____ Mercury and Venus are between the Sun and Earth.

_____ Joe poured and drank the ice water.

_____ The cow and its calf live in that pasture.

_____ Avis and Edith held and watched the sparklers.

_____ Jupiter and Saturn have rings.

_____ The machine copied and collated the reports.

_____ Larry and Dalia have braces.

_____ A tape recorder but not a CD player records and plays music.

_____ Rhett bit, chewed, and swallowed the burger.

_____ Judy cleaned and filleted the fish.

🔍 Review Work

Write an *SS* above each simple subject. Underline the simple predicates with blue.

✏️ Draft Book

Write 10 sentences with compound subjects, compound predicates, or both.

▶ Can I Stand Alone? ▷ clauses

A clause is a group of words with a subject and a predicate. An independent clause can stand alone as a sentence.

example: Jane plays baseball.

A dependent clause cannot stand alone; it is used with an independent clause.

example: because she likes the sport (not a sentence)
Jane plays baseball because she likes the sport.

Write *IC* if the group of words is an independent clause. Write *DC* if the group of words is a dependent clause.

_____ whenever Dillon gets a pickle

_____ everyone teases him

_____ jasmine rides her horse Tally

_____ so Chad bought a new bat

_____ those flowers are blooming early

_____ until Lila decides to finish her homework

_____ i walked a mile before school

_____ since it was thundering and lightning

_____ because the bag of candy was unopened

_____ kirsten chewed three sticks of gum

_____ the store closed at six o'clock

_____ if Mark orders french fries

_____ lynn hung the picture on the wall

_____ although the power went out

_____ the toilet-paper roll is empty

🔍 **Review Work**

Add uppercase letters and punctuation to the sentences above.

✏️ **Draft Book**

Write complete sentences using the dependent clauses above.

Geometry

clauses

A clause is a group of words with a subject and a predicate. An independent clause can stand alone.

> **example:**   Louis often swims.

A dependent clause cannot stand alone; it is used with an independent clause.

> **example:**   because he lives at the beach (not a sentence)
> Louis often swims because he lives at the beach.

When a dependent clause is added after an independent clause, no additional punctuation is needed. When a dependent clause is added before an independent clause, a comma is placed between the two clauses.

> **example:**   Because he lives at the beach , Louis often swims.

Underline each independent clause once. Underline each dependent clause twice. Add commas where needed.

Because I have a test tomorrow I am studying my geometry.

All closed figures with three or more straight sides are polygons, so triangles, octagons, and pentagons are polygons.

Circles and ovals do not have straight sides, so they are not polygons.

A shape is not a quadrilateral unless it has four sides.

Trapezoids, parallelograms, rectangles, and squares all have four sides so they must be quadrilaterals.

If a quadrilateral has four parallel sides, it is a parallelogram.

Because a rectangle has parallel sides it must be a parallelogram as well as a quadrilateral.

 Review Work

Circle the articles with orange.

 Draft Book

Write 10 sentences combining independent and dependent clauses. Use commas when needed.

▶ Just a Piece

phrases and clauses

A phrase is a group of words that does not have a subject and predicate. A clause is a group of words with a subject and a predicate. An independent clause can stand alone. A dependent clause cannot stand alone.

Write _P_ if the group of words is a phrase. Write _IC_ if the group of words is an independent clause. Write _DC_ if the group of words is a dependent clause.

_____ with Tom and me

_____ Doug walks

_____ whenever the news comes on television

_____ running and jumping in the leaves

_____ around nine o'clock

_____ Jill likes drawing

_____ is great at editing

_____ so that he can get his work done

_____ shimmering and sparkling in the sun

_____ sea turtles swim many miles

_____ the open bag of potato chips

_____ little striped fish

_____ although I knew the material

_____ crashing through the woods

_____ if Olive wins one more competition

_____ after Jean missed the bus

_____ this pen works

_____ Jeff mows the lawn

🔍 Review Work

Add uppercase letters and punctuation to the independent clauses above.

✏️ Draft Book

Use the phrases and dependent clauses to write complete sentences.

Name _____

▶ Stop the Run

independent clauses and conjunctions

When two independent clauses are written together, they create a run-on sentence. Two related independent clauses can be joined into one sentence with a comma and coordinating conjunction. There are seven coordinating conjunctions: *and, nor, but, for, yet, so,* and *or.*

example: Jasmine needs a nap, **or** she may fall asleep.

subject   predicate   conjunction   subject   predicate

Write an *SS* above each simple subject and underline each simple predicate.

The bluebird swooped down, but it missed the grasshopper.

Val read the ingredients on the ice-cream package, but she didn't find "milk" anywhere.

We are going skiing, and I am bringing my scarf.

Frannie gave the dog a treat, yet it is still barking.

Alvie has a test tomorrow, so she is planning to study tonight.

I knitted the scarf for Dana, but she didn't like it.

Lola didn't clean her room, so she can't leave right now.

You can choose swimming for a physical education class, or you can choose gymnastics.

The phone is ringing, yet no one has answered it.

Lola's watch is under warranty, yet the store refuses to fix it.

You can clear the table, or I can do it.

Fortoula and Melina love strawberries, so they are going to pick some tomorrow.

 Review Work

Circle the commas and coordinating conjunctions used to separate the independent clauses.

 Draft Book

Write 10 sentences that join independent clauses with commas and conjunctions.

▶ One or Two?

independent clauses and conjunctions

When two independent clauses are written together, they create a run-on sentence. To correct a run-on, decide where the first sentence ends and the second begins. The clauses can remain in one sentence if they are separated by a comma and a coordinating conjunction. There are seven coordinating conjunctions: *and, nor, but, for, yet, so,* and *or.*

example: The stars were coming out the moon wasn't up yet. =
The stars were coming out, but the moon wasn't up yet.

Separate each run-on sentence with a comma and a conjunction. Rewrite the sentences correctly on the lines.

Hannah was exhausted she had to finish her homework.

_____

Tyrone saw that man drop his wallet he returned it to him.

_____

Is that box heavy is that box light?

_____

The rain came down in a torrent it flooded the driveway.

_____

Kate kicked the ball hard she made the winning goal.

_____

We could go to the movies we could go to the arcade.

_____

I have the hiccups I am getting a glass of water.

_____

 Review Work

Underline the complete subjects once and the complete predicates twice.

 Draft Book

Write five sentences that join independent clauses with commas and conjunctions.

Name _____

When two independent clauses are written together, they create a run-on sentence. To correct a run-on, decide where the first sentence ends and the second begins. The clauses can be separated into two sentences or remain in one sentence if they are separated by a semicolon.

example: You have a cut bandage it. = You have a cut; bandage it.

Separate each run-on sentence with a semicolon. Rewrite the sentences correctly on the lines.

Walk down the hallway turn right at the end.

_____

Please quit crying you are going to be fine.

_____

Your alarm is ringing turn it off.

_____

It could snow today take your boots with you.

_____

Brandon is in my class he sits right next to me.

_____

The air show is in town we are going today.

_____

Venus is the second planet from the Sun Earth is the third planet.

_____

My nose is cold my cheeks are numb.

_____

 Review Work

Underline the pronouns with red.

 Draft Book

Write five sentences that join independent clauses with semicolons.

© Carson-Dellosa

LC1.3

Name _____

▶ Stop and Start ▶ run-on sentences

When two independent clauses are written together, they create a run-on sentence. To correct a run-on, decide where the first sentence ends and the second begins. Separate them into two sentences by adding punctuation and uppercase letters.

example: Terrence is helpful he sets the table every night. =
Terrence is helpful. He sets the table every night.

Separate these run-on sentences. Put a punctuation mark at the end of each first sentence. Cross out the lowercase letter and write the uppercase letter above it to begin each second sentence.

The flowers are beginning to bloom I think they will need water and fertilizer.

Put the spaghetti in the water is beginning to boil.

Leah is sniffling would you get her a box of tissues?

Dad went to get groceries Ian went along.

Liz is tie-dyeing a scarf she is being careful not to get the dye on her clothes.

Ralph bought a new puzzle it has 1,000 pieces.

Pablo watched that movie he said we should see it in the theater.

Brett earned ten dollars he will save it for our trip to the amusement park.

Julie putted the ball it dropped right into the hole.

Melinda and Artie helped Mrs. Porter rake her yard she is a nice woman.

The squirrel jumped onto the bird feeder it scared the birds away.

Little green blueberries are on those bushes in a month they will be ready to pick.

We picked strawberries today Mom will make strawberry shortcake for dessert.

The mail carrier dropped off a big package I wonder what's in it.

Tori and Jasmine found monarch caterpillars they were on those milkweed plants.

 Review Work

Underline the complete subjects once and the complete predicates twice.

 Draft Book

Write 10 run-on sentences. Trade with a partner and correct each run-on sentence by separating them into complete sentences.

Name _____

Breaking Apart ▶ run-on sentences

When two independent clauses are written together, they create a run-on sentence. To correct a run-on, decide where the first sentence ends and the second begins. Separate them into two sentences by adding punctuation and uppercase letters.

example: The lion is huge he looks fierce. = The lion is huge. He looks fierce.

Separate the run-on sentences. Rewrite them correctly on the lines.

Do you know what I think I think this is fun.

_____

A storm is brewing it will hit any minute.

_____

Jolene can't find her scissors she needs them to cut this paper.

_____

Louise has a dog its name is Alfie.

_____

The towels are in the washer they need to go into the dryer.

_____

Can you see the gorilla there he is in the corner.

_____

Papier-mâché is great to use the paste feels so slimy.

_____

Let me see those spots oh dear, you have chicken pox!

_____

Review Work

Underline the adjectives in the sentences.

Draft Book

Use one corrected sentence pair from above to write a story.

Name _____

▶ Depend On It

When two independent clauses are written together, they create a run-on sentence. To correct a run-on, decide where the first sentence ends and the second begins. The clauses can be separated into two sentences or remain in one sentence if one is changed to a dependent clause. When the dependent clause is added after an independent clause, no additional punctuation is needed. When the dependent clause is added before an independent clause, a comma is placed between the two clauses.

example: I am tired I am going to bed. =
I am tired, so I am going to bed. or Since I am tired, I am going to bed.

Separate each run-on sentence. For each sentence, change one independent clause to a dependent clause. Use a variety of coordinating conjunctions. Rewrite the sentences correctly on the lines.

Margo is angry she slammed the door.

_____

We can't start the movie Beth is not here yet.

_____

It is daytime the dense clouds make it look like evening.

_____

The dog walks towards her Abbie smiles.

_____

Mom is busy the phone rings.

_____

We can go we get a ride.

_____

 Review Work

Underline the nouns with yellow.

 Draft Book

Write 10 run-on sentences. Trade with a partner and correct each sentence by changing one clause to a dependent clause.

Name _____

No More Run-Ons > run-on sentences

When two independent clauses are written together, they create a run-on sentence. To correct a run-on, decide where the first sentence ends and the second begins. The clauses can be separated into two sentences or remain in one sentence if they are separated by a comma and a conjunction or a semicolon. The clauses can also remain in one sentence if one is changed to a dependent clause.

Separate each run-on sentence. Rewrite the sentences correctly on the lines. Use each option listed above at least once.

Max ran to the corner Max walked back.

_____

Jodi fixed my computer I am grateful that she did.

_____

I will bring the hose you get the sprinkler.

_____

Veronica is in the chorus Pryor is in the chorus.

_____

Mr. Frix sharpened these scissors they work great now.

_____

Kim already finished the chapter I need to finish so we can discuss it.

_____

 Review Work

Underline the complete subjects once and the complete predicates twice.

 Draft Book

Find a page of writing in your Draft Book. Use the five options above to repair any run-on sentences.

Name _____

▶ Shorten It

Abbreviations of proper nouns, special titles, and degrees are capatilized. Abbreviations of most common nouns are not capitalized. When used with a proper adjective, an abbreviation is capitalized. An abbreviation usually ends with a period.

examples: J. B. Kinard & Co.
1234 Bluebird Dr.

Write an abbreviation for each word. Capitalize when needed and add periods. A few have been done for you.

drive	_____	Saturday	_____	Senior	_____
Mister	_____	ounce	_____	General	_____
company	_____	March	_____	street	_____
Private	_____	Saint	_____	yard	yd.
Reverend	_____	avenue	Ave.	Sunday	_____
Doctor	_____	Missus	_____	inch	_____
Monday	_____	April	_____	et cetera	_____
December	_____	Thursday	_____	feet	_____
Post Office	_____	January	_____	February	_____
Friday	Fri.	August	_____	September	_____
October	_____	pound	_____	Junior	_____
Wednesday	_____	dozen	_____	November	_____
incorporated	_____	Tuesday	_____	boulevard	_____
United States	_____				

 Review Work

Draw an X next to each proper noun.

 Draft Book

Begin a list of abbreviations for future reference. Write each full word and its abbreviation.

Name _____

 # Hey!

Interjections show strong feelings or sudden emotions. They can be words or just sounds, gasps, or exclamations that are more like noises than regular words. An interjection usually comes at the beginning of a sentence, often an exclamatory sentence. It can be followed by an exclamation mark or a comma.

Common interjections: aha, ahem, goodness, gosh, gracious, gross, grr, hello, help, hey, hooray, no, nonsense, oh, oops, ouch, phew, psst, rats, shh, super, terrific, thanks, ugh, well, wow, yes, yikes, yuck

Draw a box around each interjection and the punctuation following it.

OK, I understand this now.

Shh! We're trying to get our work done.

Ouch, get off my foot!

Wow! I passed!

Mmmm, something smells delicious!

Really, would you do that for me?

Stop! That isn't very nice.

Hold on, I'm almost finished.

Oops! I broke the lead on another pencil.

Hey, give that back!

Review Work

Write an *SS* above the simple subject in each sentence. Underline the simple predicates with blue.

Draft Book

Write 10 sentences using interjections. Write some that need commas and some that need exclamation marks.

Name _____

 # Here and There

Proper nouns name special people, places, and things. When proper nouns name a city and state, a comma goes between them.

example: Orlando, Florida

Write the addresses correctly. Apply what you know about abbreviations. Capitalize all proper nouns. Put a comma between each city and state name.

mrs allison katt   _____
123 tigertail court   _____
feline city north dakota 22324   _____

dr ian w williams   _____
789 scholars way   _____
smartsville ohio 98789   _____

Add uppercase letters and commas where needed.

Mrs. Jolly's granddaughter lives in lake city michigan.

Esai got a package from seaside maine.

Erika ordered some clothing from outland montana.

Maurice sent a letter from icyville alaska to sunnyside georgia.

Pierre stayed overnight in sleepy town tennessee.

 ## Review Work

Circle the neuter nouns in the sentences above.

 ## Draft Book

Create an address page. Write the addresses of your friends, classmates, teachers, etc. Use commas, uppercase letters, and abbreviations correctly.

▶ Put in Your Commas

Commas are used in certain dates to separate the day of the week, the month and date, and the year.

yes: Saturday, March 15   no: March 15

yes: Saturday, March 15, 2003   no: March 2003

yes: March 15, 2003

Add commas where needed in the dates.

Sunday August 18 1991 _____

Wednesday February 26 _____

October 11 1973 _____

December 30 _____

Tuesday June 29 _____

May 2003 _____

July 4 1880 _____

Rewrite each sentence correctly. Write out abbreviated words.

The first practice is Sat. Sept. 3.

_____

Samuel's birthday is Feb. 15.

_____

Sasha was born Tues. Jan. 30 2001.

_____

Trish will graduate Thurs. June 11.

_____

 Review Work

Choose two dates from the first section of the page. Rewrite them using abbreviations.

_____   _____

 Draft Book

Write 10 sentences using dates. Add commas as needed.

▶ Reading and Viewing   titles

Underline the titles of books, magazines, newspapers, plays, movies, musicals, and television shows. In typed form, these titles are often italicized instead of underlined. Quotation marks go around subsets of the above: article titles, chapter titles, essays, short stories, songs, and poems. Capitalize the first and last words of a title, as well as any important words (not a preposition or article unless it is the first or last word).

Correct the titles.

Book:

walking through the waves   _____

Magazine or Newspaper:

outback times   _____

Movie:

scaring you continuously   _____

Play, Musical, or Opera:

about a town in the arctic   _____

Television Show:

let's laugh for an hour!   _____

Underline the titles in the sentences.

We watch Get a Grip every Saturday night.

Jeri and I went to the theater to see Big Time Superhero.

Madame Butterfly is my mother's favorite opera.

Can Susie read The Moon Press when you are done with it?

Orry is in a play called Now We Are Great.

 Review Work

Circle the articles with orange.

 Draft Book

Look through several pages of writing in your Draft Book and check your use of titles. Make corrections where necessary.

Name _____

▶ Now Read This ▶ quotation marks

Underline the titles of books, magazines, newspapers, plays, movies, musicals, and television shows. In typed form, these titles are often italicized instead of underlined. Quotation marks go around subsets of the above: article titles, chapter titles, essays, short stories, songs, and poems. Capitalize the first and last words of a title, as well as any important words (not a preposition or article unless it is the first or last word).

Correct the titles.

Chapter Title:

the broken arm   _____

Essay or Short Story:

how to complete your homework   _____

Song:

cricket leg serenade   _____

Poem:

no means no   _____

Put quotation marks around the titles.

Mary memorized the poem June Bug for her presentation.

Larry handed in his essay How to Handle Little Sisters.

Since he just finished Evening in September, Carlos now has only two chapters left.

This article called Of Course My Dog Ate It is funny.

Can Kassie read New Beach Opens when you are done with the paper?

If you whistle Summer Song, the dog will howl with you.

 Review Work

Circle the indefinite nouns in the sentences above.

 Draft Book

Look through several pages of writing in your Draft Book and check your use of quotation marks. Make corrections where necessary.

Name _____

The Words Said

Direct quotations are treated in a special way. The first word of a direct quotation is capitalized. Quotation marks go around the words people say. Punctuation at the end or at a break in the quote goes inside the quotation marks.

examples: Rob said, "This is fun."
"Stop that!" exclaimed Rob.
"I did not hear you. What did you say?" asked Rob.
"I like this," said Rob.

Rewrite each sentence correctly on the line. Add quotation marks, other punctuation, and uppercase letters as needed.

sen j k post declared this state is a great place

_____

hand washing prevents the spread of germs explained dr heath

_____

I am smarter than you retorted henry

_____

can i have a peanut asked jesse

_____

can't you ever quit annoying me sighed jamal

_____

she exclaimed my red pen has run out of ink

_____

would you like to have pizza questioned ryan

_____

 Review Work

Draw an X next to each proper noun that names a person.

 Draft Book

Write a sentence for each verb used instead of *said*. Put quotation marks around the words people or characters say.

▶ You Just Keep Talking ▶ quotations

Direct quotations are treated in a special way. The first word of a direct quotation is capitalized. Quotation marks go around the words people say. Punctuation at the end or at a break in the quote goes inside the quotation marks.

examples: "Since you have prepaid tickets," stated the desk clerk, "you may enter to the right."

"This is awful," sighed Bob. "Everything we typed was just lost."

Rewrite each sentence correctly on the line. Add quotation marks, other punctuation, and uppercase letters as needed.

i really think matilda insisted there is a better way

_____

put your books away stated ms glow the test begins now

_____

the mail capt m t hedd announced has arrived

_____

can't you leave me alone lacy grunted i'm busy

_____

you said we could go soon persisted beverly can we go now

_____

i wonder questioned emily why the cat won't eat the watermelon

_____

i will be on the patio explained amy reading my new book

_____

 Review Work

Draw an X next to each proper noun that names a person.

 Draft Book

Begin a list of alternate words for *said*. Refer to this list for future writing assignments.

Name _____

When a word is highlighted or a title is used inside a direct quote, single quotation marks are used.

example: Chelsea said, "I can't seem to spell the word 'peninsula' correctly in this paper."

At the end of a quote, the ending punctuation comes between the single and double quotation marks.

example: "Why can't I spell 'peninsula'?" asked Chelsea.

Rewrite each sentence correctly. Add quotation marks, single quotation marks, other punctuation, and uppercase letters as needed.

pippa said i read the article bike safety by mike b helmet

_____

would you play america the beautiful on the piano asked sadie

_____

my essay life in antarctica is due tomorrow explained ramsey

_____

how do you spell beluga questioned majaa

_____

we have to read nighttime merle complained it is the longest chapter

_____

mom said you certainly may when i asked her replied jon

_____

mr rich announced we are going to sing spring day

_____

 Review Work

Draw an X next to each proper noun that names a person. Draw a triangle next to each proper noun that names a place.

 Draft Book

Add to your list of alternate words for *said*.

Name _____

▶ Dear Friend

Letters have five parts: date, greeting, body, closing, and signature. The words in the greetings and closings begin with uppercase letters. They end with commas. Each has a line to itself.

April 5, 2002   ← date

Dear Uncle Wolf,   ← greeting

    I enjoyed riding horses at your farm. Cleaning
the stalls was rather disgusting, but I really liked grooming ← body
your horse. I can't wait to visit you again.

        Love,   ← closing
        Whitney   ← signature

Fill in the missing parts in the letter below. Include the day, month, and year in the date. Label each part.

_____   ← _____

Dear _____,   ← _____

    I went to Mrs. Walker's book reading today.
It was fun. I finished a book and borrowed another. ← body
I am going back next Tuesday. I hope you can
meet me there. Would you like to go to lunch
before the reading?

_____   ← _____

_____   ← _____

 Review Work

    Underline the nouns with yellow and the verbs
with blue in the body of the letter above.

Draft Book

    Write a letter to a friend. Include all of the parts
listed above.

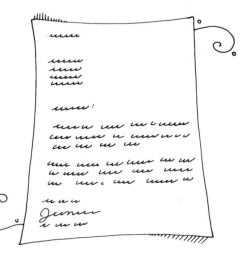

The Rules Have Changed

business letters

Business letters have seven parts: return address, date, inside address, greeting, body, closing, and signature. Business letters are usually typed, all of the information is aligned on the left, and paragraphs are separated with spaces. The return address is the letter writer's address. It includes the letter writer's name, street address, city, state, and zip code. The date appears directly below the return address. The inside address includes the name (and title, if necessary) of the person to whom the letter is being written, his or her company name, street address, city, state, and zip code. The greeting is formal and includes the person's title and last name followed by a colon. The body follows, using the format of a personal letter. The closing is also formal; *sincerely* is an appropriate word to use. The letter ends with the letter writer's full name. Business letters should be short, formal, and to the point.

Label the parts of the business letter.

miss patricia street
243 oak avenue ←_____
thisplace ohio 12345
monday october 3 2002 ←_____

mrs g h wells
chamber of commerce ←_____
33 icy avenue
colder alaska 11111

dear mrs g h wells ←_____

Hey there! I am writing this letter two request info. about
your city. mr smarts my social studies teacher said many ←_____
chamber of commerces would send info. about their towns.
I would like any materials you could send

your friend ←_____

patti ←_____

Review Work

Rewrite the letter on another sheet of paper. Make all necessary corrections.

Draft Book

Write a business letter to the Chamber of Commerce of a city you would like to visit and request information about the area and its attractions. Follow the rules for writing a business letter.

LCI.3

Name _____

▶ One Hundred Twenty-One ▶ hyphens

Hyphens are used in writing. They are used between two-part numbers from twenty-one to ninety-nine when they are written as words. Hyphens are used to write fractions as words. Hyphens are also used to break a word between syllables at the end of a line.

examples: one hundred twenty-four
one-third
im-perfect, imper-fect (not imp-erfect)

Write the numbers and fractions as words.

87 _____   39 _____

43 _____ $^1/_2$ _____

781 _____   292 _____

$^3/_4$ _____ $^9/_{10}$ _____

Hyphenate each word for division at the end of a line. If you are unsure of syllable breaks, look in a dictionary. More than one option may be possible.

conjunction _____   subject _____

predicate _____   independent _____

dependent _____   pronoun _____

interjection _____   adjective _____

adverb _____   preposition _____

quotation _____   abbreviation _____

article _____   appositive _____

⌕ Review Work

Choose one of the grammar words and draw a star beside it. Write a sentence showing an example of this word.

_____

✎ Draft Book

Choose five numbers or fractions not listed above and write them as words.

Name _____

No . . . or Yes?   double negatives

A negative word indicates *no*. When two negative words are used, the phrase becomes a positive, or *yes*, statement. This is confusing to the reader and should be avoided. Use only one negative word when you mean to indicate *no*.

examples: We can't go nowhere. (no) We can go somewhere. (yes - positive)

We can't go anywhere. or We can go nowhere. (negative)

Write the correct negative word(s) on each line.

neither, never, no, nobody, none, no one, nor, nothing, nowhere, weren't, won't

Negative Words	**Positive Opposite**
_____	were
_____	somebody, anybody
_____	or
_____	either
_____	something, anything
_____	some, any
_____	will
_____	someone, anyone
_____	yes, any, a
_____	sometimes, often, ever
_____	somewhere, anywhere

Circle the correct words to make the sentences indicate *no*.

Geraldine (will, won't) go to any practices until she is better.

I don't want (no, any) strawberry shortcake right now.

The berries are spoiled; we can do (nothing, something) with any of them.

The puppy (was, wasn't) nowhere to be seen.

 Review Work

Underline the prepositional phrases in the sentences above.

 Draft Book

Review several pages of writing in your Draft Book. Check for double negatives and make corrections where needed.

Name _____

▶ Double Trouble > double negatives

A negative word indicates *no*. When two negative words are used, the phrase becomes a positive, or *yes*, statement. This is confusing to the reader and should be avoided. Use only one negative word when you mean to indicate *no*. If a double-negative sentence contains a word like *hardly*, *barely*, or *scarcely*, change the negative word to make the sentence negative.

examples: We can't go nowhere. (no) We can go somewhere. (yes - positive)
We can't hardly go anywhere. (no) or We can hardly go anywhere. (yes - positive)

Circle the negative words in each sentence. Rewrite the sentences to indicate *no*.

There is scarcely none of the birdseed left in the feeder.

_____

Don't get no fries with your order. You can share mine.

_____

We can't stop no one from walking in the wet grass.

_____

Hardly no one ordered the pizza today.

_____

There weren't no bags of popcorn left when I got there.

_____

I don't have no money with me.

_____

It isn't barely raining outside.

_____

 Review Work

Circle the adverbs with purple.

 Draft Book

Write 10 sentences using double negatives. Trade with a partner and correct each sentence.

▶ Use Two

correlative conjunctions

Correlative conjunctions are special conjunction pairs. These pairs are split by other words. There are six correlative conjunctions: *both/and, either/or, neither/nor, whether/or, just as/so,* and *not only/but also*. The correlative conjunction *neither/nor* is not a double negative.

Circle the correlative conjunctions in each sentence.

Last night both Trey and Noreen won awards.

Whether Mom drives or Dad drives, you still need to wear your seat belt.

Elinora not only rode in a canoe, but also in a speedboat.

Neither Carlos nor Mirabel are going tonight.

Ofelia wanted to put some things in her scrapbook, but neither the map nor the itinerary fit.

Just as volcanoes erupt above ground, so they do deeply in the oceans.

We should see either belugas or minkes on this trip.

Bea not only brought the cupcakes, but also made them.

Just as cars follow street signs, so must bikes.

Either a period or a semicolon can separate a run-on sentence.

Whether it rains or not we will play soccer.

Both the paper and the project are due on Friday.

Mr. Oliver wants to know if we can either bring a binder or send two dollars for a new one.

June wants both caramel and fudge on her ice-cream sundae.

You not only need to wear your knee pads, but also your helmet.

 Review Work

Circle the infinitives in the sentences above.

 Draft Book

Write 10 sentences using correlative conjunctions from this page.

Name _____

▶ Hey, You!

A comma is used to set off the name of someone being spoken to. The comma announces to whom the speaker is talking. This is called the noun of direct address. The direct address can be added at the beginning, in the middle, or at the end of the sentence.

example: April, I would like you to call when you get there.
I would like you to call when you get there, April.
I would like you to call, April, when you get there.

Underline the person being addressed.

Walter, you must clean your room today.

I've been waiting for your call, Gerald, since you left two hours ago.

Eli and Erin went to the park, Alejandro.

Jen, do you know where the ruler is?

I'm going to watch the movie, Ian.

My room is clean and my homework is done, Dad.

This artwork is exceptional, Betsy.

Since you have been so helpful, Donna, you can call a friend.

Tara, your story is very interesting.

Write a sentence for each situation using direct address.

Tell your dog Barkie to get off the sofa.

_____

Ask your teacher when the paper is due.

_____

Tell your friend to meet you in the hallway after class.

_____

 Review Work

Draw an X next to each proper noun that names a person.

 Draft Book

Write 10 sentences using nouns of direct address.

© Carson-Dellosa

Name _____

▶ I'm Talking to You   ▷ direct address

Commas are used to set off the name of someone being spoken to. The comma announces to whom the speaker is talking. This is called the noun of direct address. Comma placement can change the meanings of some sentences.

examples: Can I call Mom? → asking someone if you can call your mother
Can I call, Mom? → asking for permission from Mom to call someone

Write the letter in front of the sentence that gives the meaning of the sentence.

A. Stop that girl Meg.   B. Stop that girl, Meg.

_____ You are asking someone to stop a girl named Meg.

_____ You are asking Meg to stop some girl.

A. I demand another, doctor.   B. I demand another doctor.

_____ You want someone to get you a different doctor.

_____ You want the doctor to give you another of something.

A. I will ask, Jade.   B. I will ask Jade.

_____ You are telling Jade you will ask someone, something.

_____ You will ask Jade something.

A. Help them push Kendal.   B. Help them push, Kendal.

_____ You are asking Kendal to help others push something.

_____ You are asking someone to help push Kendal, possibly on a sled or swing.

A. Call her Rebecca.   B. Call her, Rebecca.

_____ You are telling Rebecca to call another girl.

_____ You are telling someone to call a girl by the name Rebecca.

🔎 Review Work

Find sentences above that are not imperative sentences and draw a star next to them. Underline the subjects of the sentences with yellow.

✏️ Draft Book

Write 10 sentences using nouns of direct address.

Name _____

► Make It Interesting ► review — sentence variety

Writing is interesting when a variety of sentence structures are used. Write one of each of the following sentence types. Examples are given to help you.

1. Write a simple subject and simple predicate.
   example: Joe walks.

   _____

2. Write a simple subject and simple predicate with adjectives, articles, and/or adverbs.
   example: A tired Joe walks slowly.

   _____

3. Use an appositive.
   example: Joe, my tired little brother, walks slowly.

   _____

4. Add a direct object and possibly an indirect object.
   example: My tired little brother gives Mom a goodnight kiss.

   _____

5. Include one or more prepositions.
   example: Joe, my tired little brother, walks slowly down the hall to bed.

   _____

6. Make a compound subject and/or verb.
   example: My tired little brother kisses Mom and walks slowly to bed.

   _____

7. Use a dependent clause.
   example: When the moon came out, Joe, my little brother, kissed Mom and walked to bed.

   _____

8. Join independent clauses.
   example: My little brother kisses Mom, and he walks down the hall to bed.

   _____

9. Add conversation.
   example: "Goodnight," whispered Joe as he kissed Mom and walked to bed.

   _____

Name _____

This is the piece you began with at the beginning of your grammar study. Use it to demonstrate your improved understanding of grammar. Follow the directions on this page and page 114.

(1)Arnie studies rocks and minerals with his class. (2)The class observes rocks, performs field tests on the minerals, and reads extensively about both. (3)He discovered that there are three types of rocks: sedimentary, igneous, and metamorphic.

(4)Sedimentary rocks are formed in layers. (5)The layers are deposited in streams and riverbeds. (6)Sand, pebbles, plant matter, and animal parts can all end up in these layers. (7)Over time, the layers solidify, and sedimentary rock is formed. (8)The plant matter and animal parts become fossils.

(9)Igneous rocks are formed in, under, and around volcanoes. (10)The molten rock, or heated liquid rock, forms underground. (11)It is called magma. (12)Some magma cools slowly underground, becoming igneous rock. (13)Pressure causes other magma to rise to the surface. (14)When magma exits the volcano, its name changes to lava. (16)Lava flows from the volcano, incinerating everything it touches. (17)Finally, it cools. (18)Solidified lava is igneous rock. (19)Igneous rocks have many different looks depending on how quickly they cool. (20)Igneous rock can have air bubbles and be very light, or it can be jet black and very solid.

(21)Metamorphic rock is changed rock. (22)It forms deep underground. (23)Sedimentary or igneous rock that has been compressed by underground pressure and heat becomes metamorphic rock. (24)The heat and pressure cause the layers of sedimentary and igneous rock to become meshed together, much like the cheese in a grilled-cheese sandwich meshes slightly with the bread on each side.

(25)These three rock types are the literal building blocks of Earth. (26)They provide stability to our structures and provide many building materials for the items we use daily. (27)Arnie finds rocks fascinating.

Rewrite sentence number 27 to include a quotation.

_____

Circle the tense this article is written in:

present tense   past tense   future tense

Write the sentence number.

Find two independent clauses joined by a comma and a conjunction.   _____

Find an independent clause that precedes a dependent clause and is joined by a comma.   _____

Find a sentence that begins with a dependent clause.   _____

Look at sentence number 1. Write an *SS* above the simple subject and underline the simple predicate.

Rocks (cont.)

review

Look at sentence number 11. Underline the complete subject once and the complete predicate twice.

Find and write an example from the passage on the line. Write the sentence number behind it.

article _____

proper noun _____

common noun _____

subject pronoun _____

possessive pronoun _____

indefinite, or neutral, noun _____

compound subject _____

action verb _____

common adjective _____

demonstrative adjective _____

adverb _____

helping verb _____

linking verb + predicate noun _____

infinitive _____

direct object _____

object of the preposition _____

appositive _____

On a separate piece of paper, write a business letter to Ms. Jade Opal requesting information about joining the Rock and Mineral Club.

▶ Student Editing Checklist

Check each highlighted item*

☐ Each sentence has a complete subject and a complete predicate.

☐ Run-on sentences are avoided.

☐ Sentence variety is used.

☐ Phrases and dependent clauses are not used as sentences.

☐ Subjects agree with verbs and pronouns.

☐ Double negatives are corrected.

☐ The first letter in each sentence is capitalized, including the first letter inside quotation marks.

☐ The pronoun I is always capitalized.

☐ Each word that names a day, month, or holiday starts with an uppercase letter.

☐ Each proper noun starts with an uppercase letter.

☐ Each title starts with an uppercase letter.

☐ Quotations follow correct format for punctuation and capitalization.

☐ Friendly and business letters follow correct format.

☐ Each declarative sentence ends with a period.

☐ Each imperative sentence ends with a period or exclamation mark.

☐ Each interrogative sentence ends with a question mark.

☐ Each exclamatory sentence ends with an exclamation mark.

☐ Commas are used to separate dates.

☐ Commas are used in the greeting and closing in a friendly letter.

☐ A comma is used between a city and state.

☐ A dependent clause that precedes an independent clause is followed by a comma.

☐ Two independent clauses are joined with a conjunction and a comma.

☐ Abbreviations end with periods.

☐ Quotation marks are used around direct quotations, and certain titles.

☐ Book titles are underlined.

* Teacher highlights items for individual student editing.

Name _____

▶ Student Editing Checklist (cont.)

☐ Hyphens are used in numbers, fractions, and syllables at the ends of lines.

☐ A plural noun usually ends in *s* or *es*.

☐ A possessive noun usually ends in *'s*.

☐ Subject pronouns come before verbs.

☐ Object pronouns come after verbs.

☐ Possessive pronouns take the place of possessive nouns.

☐ Indefinite pronouns refer to nouns in a general way.

☐ Intensive pronouns draw attention to nouns or pronouns.

☐ Reflexive pronouns reflect back to the subjects of sentences.

☐ All verb tenses correctly describe when something is happening.

☐ Singular verbs follow singular nouns.

☐ Plural verbs follow plural nouns.

☐ Words are spelled correctly for their meanings.

☐ Articles are used before nouns or adjective/noun combinations.

☐ Apostrophes take the place of dropped letters in contractions.

☐ Other: _____

* Teacher highlights items for individual student editing.

Answer Key

Page 6

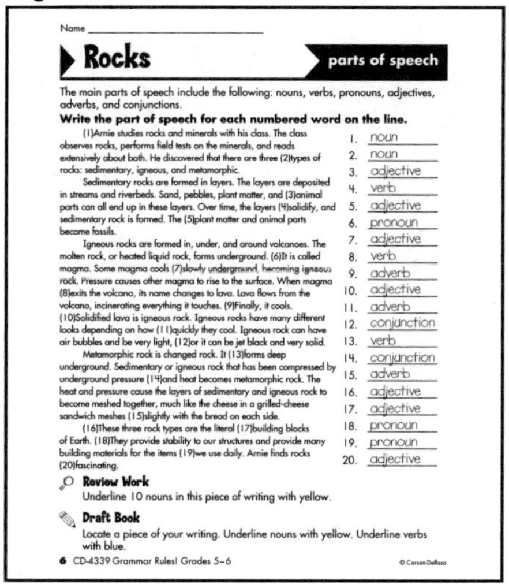

Name ____________

Rocks parts of speech

The main parts of speech include the following: nouns, verbs, pronouns, adjectives, adverbs, and conjunctions.

Write the part of speech for each numbered word on the line.

(1)Arnie studies rocks and minerals with his class. The class observes rocks, performs field tests on the minerals, and reads extensively about both. He discovered that there are three (2)types of rocks: sedimentary, igneous, and metamorphic.

Sedimentary rocks are formed in layers. The layers are deposited in streams and riverbeds. Sand, pebbles, plant matter, and (3)animal parts can all end up in these layers. Over time, the layers (4)solidify, and sedimentary rock is formed. The (5)plant matter and animal parts become fossils.

Igneous rocks are formed in, under, and around volcanoes. The molten rock, or heated liquid rock, forms underground. (6)It is called magma. Some magma cools (7)slowly underground, becoming igneous rock. Pressure causes other magma to rise to the surface. When magma (8)exits the volcano, its name changes to lava. Lava flows from the volcano, incinerating everything it touches. (9)Finally, it cools. (10)Solidified lava is igneous rock. Igneous rocks have many different looks depending on how (11)quickly they cool. Igneous rock can have air bubbles and be very light, (12)or it can be jet black and very solid.

Metamorphic rock is changed rock. It (13)forms deep underground. Sedimentary or igneous rock that has been compressed by underground pressure (14)and heat becomes metamorphic rock. The heat and pressure cause the layers of sedimentary and igneous rock to become meshed together, much like the cheese in a grilled-cheese sandwich meshes (15)slightly with the bread on each side.

(16)These three rock types are the literal (17)building blocks of Earth. (18)They provide stability to our structures and provide many building materials for the items (19)we use daily. Arnie finds rocks (20)fascinating.

1. noun
2. noun
3. adjective
4. verb
5. adjective
6. pronoun
7. adjective
8. verb
9. adverb
10. adjective
11. adverb
12. conjunction
13. verb
14. conjunction
15. adverb
16. adjective
17. adjective
18. pronoun
19. pronoun
20. adjective

Review Work
Underline 10 nouns in this piece of writing with yellow.

Draft Book
Locate a piece of your writing. Underline nouns with yellow. Underline verbs with blue.

6 CD-4339 Grammar Rules! Grades 5–6 © Carson-Dellosa

RW: Answers will vary. DB: Answers will vary.

Page 7

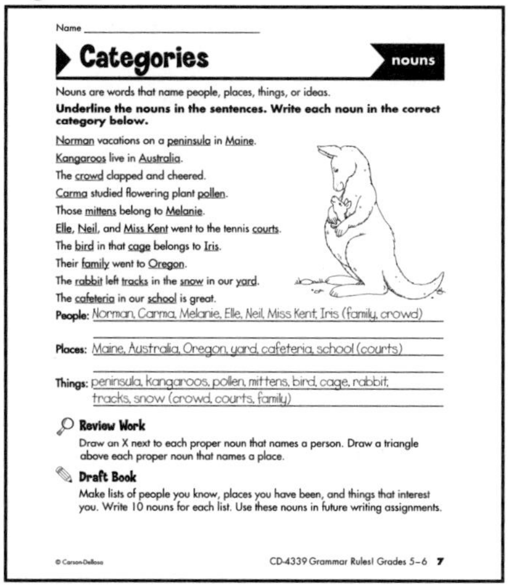

Name ____________

Categories nouns

Nouns are words that name people, places, things, or ideas.

Underline the nouns in the sentences. Write each noun in the correct category below.

Norman vacations on a peninsula in Maine.
Kangaroos live in Australia.
The crowd clapped and cheered.
Carma studied flowering plant pollen.
Those mittens belong to Melanie.
Elle, Neil, and Miss Kent went to the tennis courts.
The bird in that cage belongs to Iris.
Their family went to Oregon.
The rabbit left tracks in the snow in our yard.
The cafeteria in our school is great.

People: Norman, Carma, Melanie, Elle, Neil, Miss Kent, Iris (family, crowd)

Places: Maine, Australia, Oregon, yard, cafeteria, school (courts)

Things: peninsula, kangaroos, pollen, mittens, bird, cage, rabbit, tracks, snow (crowd, courts, family)

Review Work
Draw an X next to each proper noun that names a person. Draw a triangle above each proper noun that names a place.

Draft Book
Make lists of people you know, places you have been, and things that interest you. Write 10 nouns for each list. Use these nouns in future writing assignments.

© Carson-Dellosa CD-4339 Grammar Rules! Grades 5–6 7

RW: Draw an X next to Norman, Carma, Melanie, Elle, Neil, Miss Kent, and Iris. Draw a triangle above Maine, Australia, and Oregon. DB: Answers will vary.

Page 8

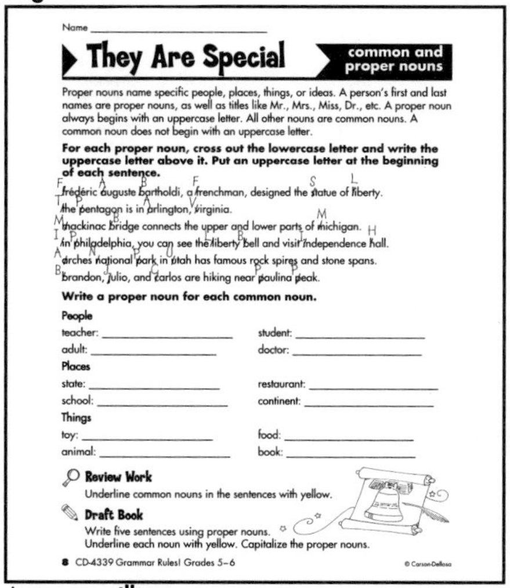

Name ____________

They Are Special common and proper nouns

Proper nouns name specific people, places, things, or ideas. A person's first and last names are proper nouns, as well as titles like Mr., Mrs., Miss, Dr., etc. A proper noun always begins with an uppercase letter. All other nouns are common nouns. A common noun does not begin with an uppercase letter.

For each proper noun, cross out the lowercase letter and write the uppercase letter above it. Put an uppercase letter at the beginning of each sentence.

frédéric auguste bartholdi, a frenchman, designed the statue of liberty.
the pentagon is in arlington, virginia.
mackinac bridge connects the upper and lower parts of michigan.
in philadelphia, you can see the liberty bell and visit independence hall.
arches national park in utah has famous rock spires and stone spans.
brandon, julio, and carlos are hiking near paulina peak.

Write a proper noun for each common noun.

People
teacher: ______ student: ______
adult: ______ doctor: ______
Places
state: ______ restaurant: ______
school: ______ continent: ______
Things
toy: ______ food: ______
animal: ______ book: ______

Review Work
Underline common nouns in the sentences with yellow.

Draft Book
Write five sentences using proper nouns. Underline each noun with yellow. Capitalize the proper nouns.

8 CD-4339 Grammar Rules! Grades 5–6 © Carson-Dellosa

Answers will vary.
RW: Underline parts, spires, and spans with yellow. DB: Answers will vary.

Page 9

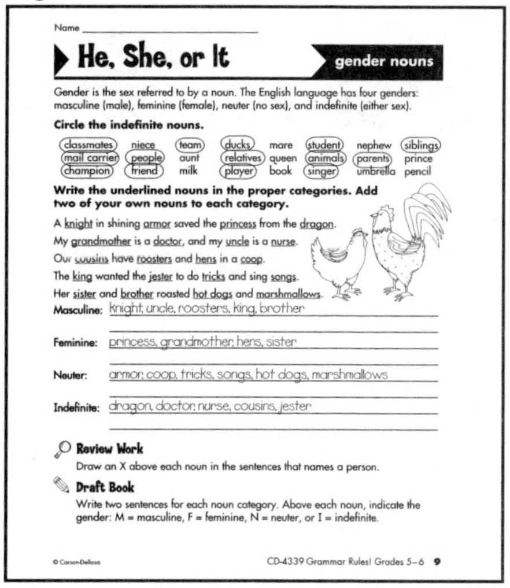

Name ____________

He, She, or It gender nouns

Gender is the sex referred to by a noun. The English language has four genders: masculine (male), feminine (female), neuter (no sex), and indefinite (either sex).

Circle the indefinite nouns.

(classmates) niece (team) (ducks) mare (student) nephew (siblings)
(mail carrier) (people) aunt (relatives) queen (animals) (parents) prince
(champion) (friend) milk (player) book (singer) umbrella pencil

Write the underlined nouns in the proper categories. Add two of your own nouns to each category.

A knight in shining armor saved the princess from the dragon.
My grandmother is a doctor, and my uncle is a nurse.
Our cousins have roosters and hens in a coop.
The king wanted the jester to do tricks and sing songs.
Her sister and brother roasted hot dogs and marshmallows.

Masculine: knight, uncle, roosters, king, brother
Feminine: princess, grandmother, hens, sister
Neuter: armor, coop, tricks, songs, hot dogs, marshmallows
Indefinite: dragon, doctor, nurse, cousins, jester

Review Work
Draw an X above each noun in the sentences that names a person.

Draft Book
Write two sentences for each noun category. Above each noun, indicate the gender: M = masculine, F = feminine, N = neuter, or I = indefinite.

© Carson-Dellosa CD-4339 Grammar Rules! Grades 5–6 9

RW: Draw an X above knight, princess, grandmother, doctor, uncle, nurse, cousins, king, jester, sister, and brother.
DB: Answers will vary.

Page 10

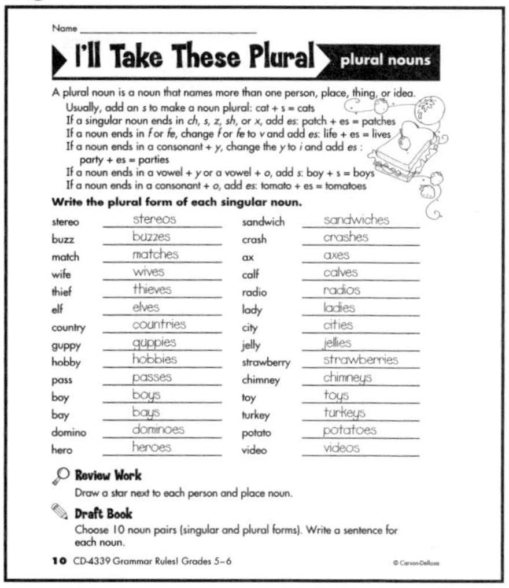

Name ____________

I'll Take These Plural plural nouns

A plural noun is a noun that names more than one person, place, thing, or idea.
Usually, add an *s* to make a noun plural: cat + s = cats
If a singular noun ends in *ch, s, z, sh,* or *x,* add *es*: patch + es = patches
If a noun ends in *f* or *fe,* change *f* or *fe* to *v* and add *es*: life + es = lives
If a noun ends in a consonant + *y,* change the *y* to *i* and add *es*: party + es = parties
If a noun ends in a vowel + *y* or a vowel + *o,* add *s*: boy + s = boys
If a noun ends in a consonant + *o,* add *es*: tomato + es = tomatoes

Write the plural form of each singular noun.

stereo	stereos	sandwich	sandwiches
buzz	buzzes	crash	crashes
match	matches	ax	axes
wife	wives	calf	calves
thief	thieves	radio	radios
elf	elves	lady	ladies
country	countries	city	cities
guppy	guppies	jelly	jellies
hobby	hobbies	strawberry	strawberries
pass	passes	chimney	chimneys
boy	boys	toy	toys
bay	bays	turkey	turkeys
domino	dominoes	potato	potatoes
hero	heroes	video	videos

Review Work
Draw a star next to each person and place noun.

Draft Book
Choose 10 noun pairs (singular and plural forms). Write a sentence for each noun.

10 CD-4339 Grammar Rules! Grades 5–6 © Carson-Dellosa

RW: Draw a star next to wives, thieves, countries, boys, bays, heroes, ladies, and cities. DB: Answers will vary.

Page 11

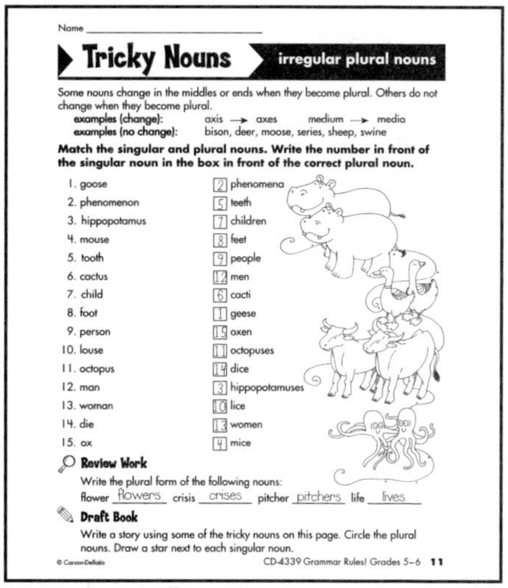

Name ____________

Tricky Nouns irregular plural nouns

Some nouns change in the middles or ends when they become plural. Others do not change when they become plural.
examples (change): axis → axes medium → media
examples (no change): bison, deer, moose, series, sheep, swine

Match the singular and plural nouns. Write the number in front of the singular noun in the box in front of the correct plural noun.

1. goose	[2] phenomena
2. phenomenon	[5] teeth
3. hippopotamus	[7] children
4. mouse	[8] feet
5. tooth	[9] people
6. cactus	[12] men
7. child	[6] cacti
8. foot	[1] geese
9. person	[15] oxen
10. louse	[11] octopuses
11. octopus	[14] dice
12. man	[3] hippopotamuses
13. woman	[10] lice
14. die	[13] women
15. ox	[4] mice

Review Work
Write the plural form of the following nouns:
flower flowers crisis crises pitcher pitchers life lives

Draft Book
Write a story using some of the tricky nouns on this page. Circle the plural nouns. Draw a star next to each singular noun.

© Carson-Dellosa CD-4339 Grammar Rules! Grades 5–6 11

DB: Answers will vary.

Page 12

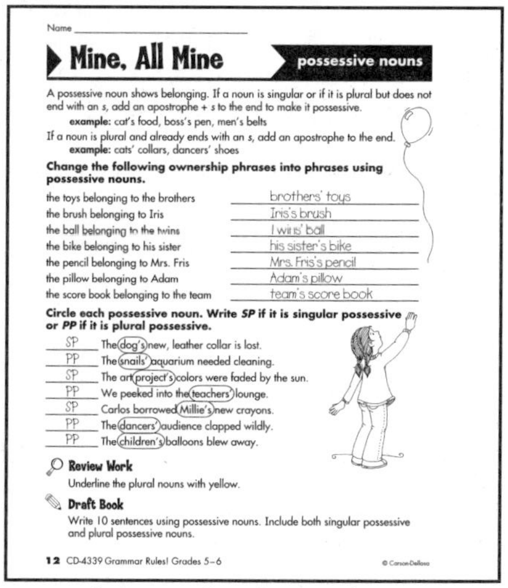

Name ____________

Mine, All Mine possessive nouns

A possessive noun shows belonging. If a noun is singular or if it is plural but does not end with an *s,* add an apostrophe + *s* to the end to make it possessive.
example: cat's food, boss's pen, men's belts
If a noun is plural and already ends with an *s,* add an apostrophe to the end.
example: cats' collars, dancers' shoes

Change the following ownership phrases into phrases using possessive nouns.

the toys belonging to the brothers	brothers' toys
the brush belonging to Iris	Iris's brush
the ball belonging to the twins	twins' ball
the bike belonging to his sister	his sister's bike
the pencil belonging to Mrs. Fris	Mrs. Fris's pencil
the pillow belonging to Adam	Adam's pillow
the score book belonging to the team	team's score book

Circle each possessive noun. Write *SP* if it is singular possessive or *PP* if it is plural possessive.

SP The (dog's) new, leather collar is lost.
PP The (snails') aquarium needed cleaning.
SP The art (project's) colors were faded by the sun.
PP We peeked into the (teachers') lounge.
SP Carlos borrowed (Millie's) new crayons.
PP The (dancers') audience clapped wildly.
PP The (children's) balloons blew away.

Review Work
Underline the plural nouns with yellow.

Draft Book
Write 10 sentences using possessive nouns. Include both singular possessive and plural possessive nouns.

12 CD-4339 Grammar Rules! Grades 5–6 © Carson-Dellosa

RW: Underline snails, colors, teachers, crayons, dancers, children, and balloons with yellow.
DB: Answers will vary.

Page 13

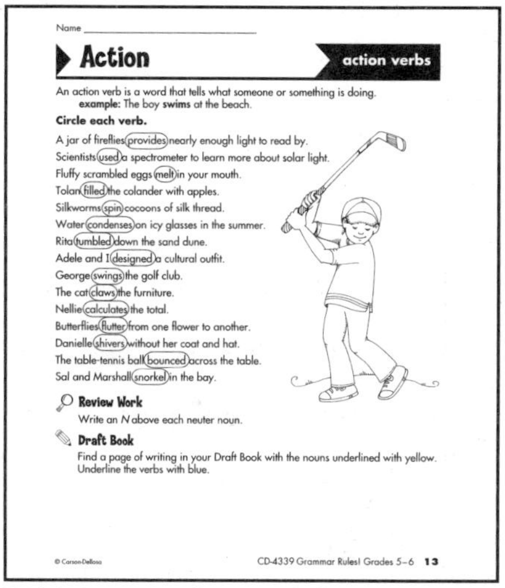

Name ____________

Action action verbs

An action verb is a word that tells what someone or something is doing.
example: The boy swims at the beach.

Circle each verb.

A jar of fireflies (provides) nearly enough light to read by.
Scientists (used) a spectrometer to learn more about solar light.
Fluffy scrambled eggs (melt) in your mouth.
Tolan (filled) the colander with apples.
Silkworms (spin) cocoons of silk thread.
Water (condenses) on icy glasses in the summer.
Rita (tumbled) down the sand dune.
Adele and I (designed) a cultural outfit.
George (swings) the golf club.
The cat (claws) the furniture.
Nellie (calculates) the total.
Butterflies (flutter) from one flower to another.
Danielle (shivers) without her coat and hat.
The table-tennis ball (bounced) across the table.
Sal and Marshall (snorkel) in the bay.

Review Work
Write an *N* above each neuter noun.

Draft Book
Find a page of writing in your Draft Book with the nouns underlined with yellow. Underline the verbs with blue.

© Carson-Dellosa CD-4339 Grammar Rules! Grades 5–6 13

RW: Write an N above jar, light, spectrometer, light, eggs, mouth, colander, apples, cocoons, thread, water, glasses, summer, dune, outfit, club, furniture, total, flower, coat, hat, ball, table, and bay. DB: Answers will vary.

Page 14

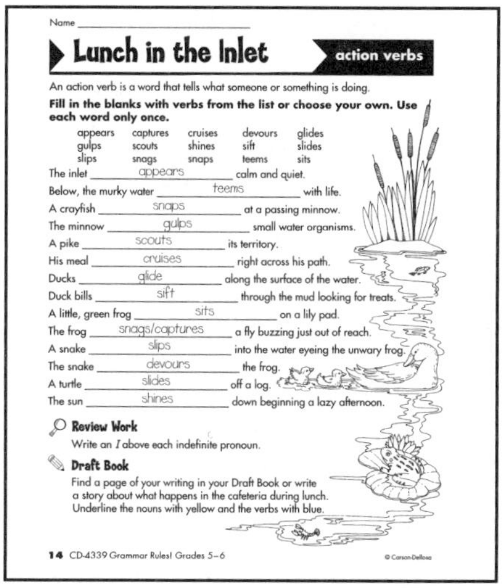

Name ____________

Lunch in the Inlet action verbs

An action verb is a word that tells what someone or something is doing.

Fill in the blanks with verbs from the list or choose your own. Use each word only once.

appears captures cruises devours glides
gulps scouts shines sift slides
slips snags snaps teems sits

The inlet appears calm and quiet.
Below, the murky water teems with life.
A crayfish snaps at a passing minnow.
The minnow gulps small water organisms.
A pike scouts its territory.
His meal cruises right across his path.
Ducks glide along the surface of the water.
Duck bills sift through the mud looking for treats.
A little, green frog sits on a lily pad.
The frog snags/captures a fly buzzing just out of reach.
A snake slips into the water eyeing the unwary frog.
The snake devours the frog.
A turtle slides off a log.
The sun shines down beginning a lazy afternoon.

Review Work
Write an *I* above each indefinite pronoun.

Draft Book
Find a page of your writing in your Draft Book or write a story about what happens in the cafeteria during lunch. Underline the nouns with yellow and the verbs with blue.

14 CD-4339 Grammar Rules! Grades 5–6 © Carson-Dellosa

Page 14 (cont.)
RW: Write I above crayfish, minnow, minnow, organisms, pike, ducks, frog, frog, fly, snake, frog, snake, and turtle.
DB: Answers will vary.

Page 15

▶ Give a Helping Hand | helping verbs/verb phrases

Helping verbs are verbs that help main verbs express tense. There are 23 helping verbs. A verb phrase acts as a single verb and is used with one or more helping verbs. Up to three helping verbs can precede the main verb. *Would, should, shall,* and *will* are helping verbs. Forms of the following verbs are also helping verbs:

be: am, are, is, was, were, be, being, been
do: do, does, did
have: have, has, had
may: may, must, might
can: can, could

Circle the helping verbs. Underline the verb phrases.

The fleas did jump through the cat's fur.
The water is pouring into the basement.
The ant had scurried into the anthill.
We are going to the amusement park.
I am excited to be here.
The lights can be dimmed with this switch.
Max was entitled to his turn.
The puppy must have tried to jump onto the bed.
That jam would make a good ice-cream topping.
The bird had flown into the bushes.
We should weed the garden before it gets too hot.
The tickets may cost too much.
Emma's family might go to the zoo tomorrow.

🔎 **Review Work**
Underline the nouns with yellow.

✏️ **Draft Book**
Write 10 sentences that use helping verbs. Circle the helping verbs. Underline the verb phrases with blue.

© Carson-Dellosa   CD-4339 Grammar Rules! Grades 5-6 **15**

RW: Underline fleas, cat's, fur, water, basement, ant, anthill, amusement park, lights, switch, Max, turn, puppy, bed, jam, topping, bird, bushes, garden, tickets, Emma's, family, and zoo with yellow.
DB: Answers will vary.

Page 16

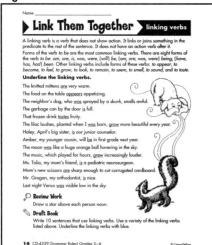

▶ Link Them Together | linking verbs

A linking verb is a verb that does not show action. It links or joins something in the predicate to the rest of the sentence. It does not have an action verb after it. Forms of the verb *to be* are the most common linking verbs. There are eight forms of the verb *to be*: am, are, is, was, were, (will) be, (am, are, was, were) being, (have, has, had) been. Other linking verbs include forms of these verbs: *to appear, to become, to feel, to grow, to look, to remain, to seem, to smell, to sound,* and *to taste.*

Underline the linking verbs.

The knitted mittens are very warm.
The food on the table appears appetizing.
The neighbor's dog, who was sprayed by a skunk, smells awful.
The garbage can by the door is full.
That frozen drink tastes fruity.
The lilac bushes, planted when I was born, grow more beautiful every year.
Haley, April's big sister, is our junior counselor.
Amber, my younger cousin, will be in first grade next year.
The moon was like a huge orange ball hovering in the sky.
The music, which played for hours, grew increasingly louder.
Ms. Tolio, my mom's friend, is a pediatric neurosurgeon.
Mom's new scissors are sharp enough to cut corrugated cardboard.
Mr. Grogan, my orthodontist, is nice.
Last night Venus was visible low in the sky.

🔎 **Review Work**
Draw a star above each person noun.

✏️ **Draft Book**
Write 10 sentences that use linking verbs. Use a variety of the linking verbs listed above. Underline the linking verbs with blue.

16 CD-4339 Grammar Rules! Grades 5-6   © Carson-Dellosa

RW: Draw a star above neighbor's, Haley, April's, sister, counselor, Amber, cousin, Ms. Tolio, mom's, friend, neurosurgeon, Mom's, Mr. Grogan, and orthodontist.
DB: Answers will vary.

Page 17

▶ Choose the Verb | noun and verb agreement

A singular noun uses a verb with an *s* at the end. A plural noun uses a verb that does not have an *s* at the end.
examples: The boy climbs the tree.
The boys climb the tree.
A verb uses the same rules as a noun when adding *s* or *es.*
Usually, add an *s* to a verb: run + s = runs
If a verb ends in *sh, s, z, ch,* or *x,* add *es:* pitch + es = pitches
If a verb ends in a consonant + *y,* change *y* to *i* and add *es:* try - y + i + es = tries
If a verb ends in a vowel + *y,* add *s:* enjoy + s = enjoys

Circle the correct verbs.

Blair (stare, stares) at the massive mess in her room.
Jade and I (catch) catches) outfield balls.
Students (choose) chooses) which vegetables to eat.
Numerous plants (thrive) thrives) in the rain forest.
People (access) accesses) the Internet.
Not many minnows (survive) survives) to become adult fish.
Darryl (complain, complains) about mowing the lawn.
Squirrels (flee) flees) when my sister opens the sliding door.
Santos (invite, invites) his friends to a sleepover.
Juan and Doug (agree) agrees) on the answer.
Our kites (fly, flies) through the air at the beach.
Mother (halt, halves) the candy bar for us to share.
Kara (spread, spreads) jelly onto the peanut butter sandwich.

🔎 **Review Work**
Draw an X above each proper noun in the sentences that names a person.

✏️ **Draft Book**
Choose five of the sentences. Rewrite each one so that the first noun is the opposite (singular or plural) of what it is now. Rewrite the verb to agree with the new subject.

© Carson-Dellosa   CD-4339 Grammar Rules! Grades 5-6 **17**

RW: Draw an X above Blair, Jade, Darryl, Santos, Juan, Doug, Mother, and Kara.
DB: Answers will vary.

Page 18

▶ Subjects | simple subject of a sentence

The simple subject of a sentence is the noun that the sentence is about.
example: Pat's fish swam in the aquarium.
example: Mount Everest is the tallest mountain in the world.
Underline the noun that is the simple subject of each sentence.

Most tree branches grow at an acute angle from the tree trunk.
The penny rolled under the cabinet.
Chan's watch was slow by an hour.
The thermometer read 62 degrees Fahrenheit.
The Marianas Trench is deeper than Mount Everest is tall.
Mount Rushmore towers over the valley.
The praying mantis is related to the cockroach.
My mom made homemade strawberry jam.
Ladybugs assist farmers by eating harmful insects.
Garnet is the January birthstone.
Abigail vacationed in California.
Parrots require lots of attention.
Bamboo is not a tree.
Paul teased Talia about the food in her lunch.

🔎 **Review Work**
Circle the plural nouns.

✏️ **Draft Book**
Find a full page of writing in your Draft Book or write a story about your favorite hobby or sport. Write an SS above the simple subject in each sentence.

18 CD-4339 Grammar Rules! Grades 5-6   © Carson-Dellosa

RW: Circle branches, degrees, ladybugs, insects, and parrots.
DB: Answers will vary.

Page 19:
Answers will vary.
RW: Underline drawing, ingredient, meal, trees, table, homes, flower, places, backyard, everything, task, plants, park, and snack with yellow. DB: Answers will vary.

Page 20

▶ Pick the Pronoun | subject pronouns

A pronoun takes the place of a noun. Subject pronouns take the place of simple subject nouns. They are *I, you, he, she, we, they,* and *it.*
Above each set of nouns, write the pronoun that could take each word's place. Add four nouns to each list.

it	she
peninsula	Aunt Amy
monorail	Darla
dog	Mrs. Stamey
television	Mother

they	we
the choir	George and I
Tim and Meg	my brother and I
the team	my class and I
the customers	you and I

he	
Mr. Foote	
the king	
Uncle Joe	
Tom	

Replace the words in bold type with subject pronouns. Write the correct pronoun on each line.

Ken removed the fender and repaired it.   He
The moon is full and bright tonight.   It
Gary and I invented a new sandwich.   We
Raccoons raided our garbage can.   They
Mrs. Berrier gave us a pop quiz today.   She

🔎 **Review Work**
Underline the nouns in the sentences above with yellow.

✏️ **Draft Book**
Find a page of writing in your Draft Book. Change the subject nouns to subject pronouns.

20 CD-4339 Grammar Rules! Grades 5-6   © Carson-Dellosa

RW: Underline Ken, fender, moon, Gary, sandwich, raccoons, can, Mrs. Berrier, and pop quiz with yellow. DB: Answers will vary.

Page 21

▶ Doing What? | simple predicate

The simple predicate is the main verb of the sentence that tells what someone or something is doing.
Underline each simple predicate.

San panicked when he noticed his lunch money missing.
The aurora borealis shimmered across the night sky.
Monarch caterpillars devour milkweed leaves.
Mosquitoes transmit malaria.
Crystie grabbed the swing with both hands.
The monkey turned around.
Rick bowled his fifth strike in a row.
The roller coaster catapulted its riders forward.
Tears poured from their eyes.
Annie and Sarah gathered the blankets.
Dean completed the order form.
He soaked them with the hose.
Mr. Roark answered their questions.
Mannie and I counted the money.

🔎 **Review Work**
Write an SS above the simple subject in each sentence.

✏️ **Draft Book**
Use one of the sentences on this page in a story. Underline the simple predicates with blue.

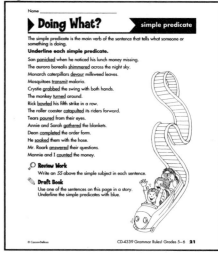

© Carson-Dellosa   CD-4339 Grammar Rules! Grades 5-6 **21**

RW: Write an SS above San, aurora borealis, caterpillars, mosquitoes, Crystie, monkey, Rick, roller coaster, tears, Annie, Sarah, Dean, he, Mr. Roark, Mannie, and I. DB: Answers will vary.

Page 22

▶ The Animal World | simple subjects and predicates

The simple subject of a sentence is the noun that the sentence is about. The simple predicate is the verb that tells what someone or something is doing.
Underline each simple subject once. Underline each simple predicate twice.

An owl watches.
Worms burrow.
An orca surfaces.
Moths flutter.
An elephant trumpets.
The spider on the web captures an unwary fly.
The gazelles stampede across the plains.
Koalas climb to the top of gum trees to eat eucalyptus leaves.
The soaring hawk scans the land for small rodents.
A red fox slinks through the underbrush towards the rabbit.

Write the plural nouns with their verbs.

worms burrow	gazelles stampede
moths flutter	koalas climb

Write the singular nouns with their verbs.

owl watches	spider captures
orca surfaces	hawk scans
elephant trumpets	red fox slinks

🔎 **Review Work**
Underline the other nouns in the sentences with yellow.

✏️ **Draft Book**
Begin a verb list. Record interesting verbs for use in future writing assignments.

22 CD-4339 Grammar Rules! Grades 5-6   © Carson-Dellosa

RW: Underline web, fly, plains, gum trees, leaves, land, rodents, underbrush, and rabbit with yellow. DB: Answers will vary.

Answer Key

Page 23

Name ____________________

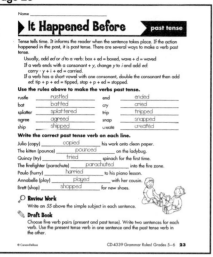

It Happened Before — past tense

Tense tells time. It informs the reader when the sentence takes place. If the action happened in the past, it is past tense. There are several ways to make a verb past tense.

Usually, add *ed* or *d* to a verb: box + ed = boxed, wave + d = waved

If a verb ends with a consonant + *y*, change *y* to *i* and add *ed*: carry - y + i + ed = carried.

If a verb has a short vowel with one consonant, double the consonant then add *ed*: tip + p + ed = tipped, stop + p + ed = stopped.

Use the rules above to make the verbs past tense.

rustle	rustled	end	ended
bat	batted	cry	cried
splatter	splattered	trip	tripped
agree	agreed	snap	snapped
ship	shipped	create	created

Write the correct past tense verb on each line.

Julio (copy) copied his work onto clean paper.
The kitten (pounce) pounced on the ladybug.
Quincy (try) tried spinach for the first time.
The firefighter (parachute) parachuted into the fire zone.
Paulo (hurry) hurried to his piano lesson.
Annabelle (play) played with her cousin.
Brett (shop) shopped for new shoes.

Review Work
Write an *SS* above the simple subject in each sentence.

Draft Book
Choose five verb pairs (present and past tense). Write two sentences for each verb. Use the present tense verb in one sentence and the past tense verb in the other.

© Carson-Dellosa CD-4339 Grammar Rules! Grades 5–6 **23**

RW: Write an SS above Julio, kitten, Quincy, firefighter, Paulo, Annabelle, and Brett.
DB: Answers will vary.

Page 24

Name ____________________

Now or Then — past and present tense

Tense tells time. When it happened in the past, it is past tense. When something happens now, it is present tense.

Underline the verb in each first sentence. Write the past tense of the verb in each second sentence.

Children crawl through the obstacle course.
Yesterday, they crawled through by the hundreds.
Mosquitoes bother the horses.
They bothered the dogs last week.
Hector bounces on the trampoline.
He bounced on it with Andy earlier.
Meg and I roll the cookie dough very carefully.
We rolled enough dough to make six dozen cookies.
The doctor inoculates the child.
She inoculated several children this morning.
Tara and Nell drift along on the inner tubes.
They drifted downstream.
The news helicopter hovers over the scene.
It hovered there until the photos were taken.
Mark tastes the broccoli salad.
He tasted the artichoke dip earlier.

Review Work
Underline the subject nouns in the first sentences with yellow. Underline the pronouns that replaced them in the second sentences with red.

Draft Book
Find a story you wrote in your Draft Book. Put boxes around verbs with *ed* endings.

24 CD-4339 Grammar Rules! Grades 5–6 © Carson-Dellosa

RW: Underline children, mosquitoes, Hector, Meg and I, doctor, Tara and Nell, helicopter, and Mark with yellow. Underline they, they, he, we, she, they, it, and he with red.
DB: Answers will vary.

Page 25

Name ____________________

Now and Then — past and present tense

Tense tells time. It informs the reader when the sentence takes place. One way to make a verb past tense is to add *ed* to the end.
past tense: Sam **studied** for the test.
present tense: Sam **studies** for the test.
An irregular verb becomes past tense by changing its spelling.
example: catch/caught, shine/shone, sting/stung

Circle the simple predicate. Identify the tense of the verb by writing *past* or *present* on the line.

Bees (buzz) around the daisies. present
Maddie (brushes) sand from her legs. present
Kali (ate) ice cream. past
The parakeet (nibbled) on crackers. past
Fiona (bandages) the cut on her knee. present
Cameron (sharpened) his pencils for the test. past
Kris (disturbs) the teacher. present
Brad and Jeremy (left) the theater. past
The hamsters (race) around their cages. present
Andy (wrote) a great acrostic poem. past
Sally (photographs) our field trips. present
My brother (taught) me to tie my shoes. past
Willie (shovels) sand into the sandbox. present
Jennifer (threw) hay into the horse stalls. past
Dillon (cried) for his bottle. past

Review Work
Write an *SS* above each simple subject.

Draft Book
Write five sentences using present tense verbs and five sentences using past tense verbs.

© Carson-Dellosa CD-4339 Grammar Rules! Grades 5–6 **25**

Page 25 (cont.)

RW: Write an SS above bees, Maddie, Kali, parakeet, Fiona, Cameron, Kris, Brad, Jeremy, hamsters, Andy, Sally, brother, Willie, Jennifer, and Dillon.
DB: Answers will vary.

Page 26

Name ____________________

Things to Come — future tense

Tense tells time. It informs the reader when the sentence takes place. To make a verb future tense, add the helping verb *will* before the singular present tense form of the verb. If the verb has an ending, drop it before adding *will*.
example: Bob **rakes** the lawn. Bob **will rake** the lawn.
Jan **ate** the apple. Jan **will eat** the apple.

Write the correct future tense verb on each line.

Jeremy (builds) will build a birdhouse.
Allie (caught) will catch some fish.
The boat (cruises) will cruise around the channel.
Blake and Rico (jumped) will jump into the pool.
The class (observes) will observe the plants as they grow.
Jess (painted) will paint that set of chairs.
The monkey (grabbed) will grab the rope.
Quinn (helped) will help make the cake.
Sydney (completed) will complete the book.
A dolphin (bumps) will bump the boat gently.
Jordi (brought) will bring cupcakes for the party.
The sauce (burns) will burn with the burner on high.
Sukie (carries) will carry the blueberries to the car.
Ian, Marshall, and Jacob (threw) will throw water balloons.
The silverware (clatters) will clatter to the floor.

Review Work
Underline the nouns with yellow.

Draft Book
Write about an imaginary trip using future tense verbs.

26 CD-4339 Grammar Rules! Grades 5–6 © Carson-Dellosa

RW: Underline Jeremy, birdhouse, Allie, fish, boat, channel, Blake, Rico, pool, class, plants, Jess, set, chairs, monkey, rope, Quinn, cake, Sydney, book, dolphin, boat, Jordi, cupcakes, party, sauce, burner, Sukie, blueberries, car, Ian, Marshall, Jacob, balloons, silverware, and floor with yellow.
DB: Answers will vary.

Page 27

Name ____________________

Past, Present, or Future — verb tenses

Verbs use tenses to tell when something is happening.

Underline the verbs. If a verb is future tense, underline both the main verb and the helping verb *will*. Circle past, present, or future.

The barrel collects rainwater.	past	(present)	future
Jamie writes to her friend.	past	(present)	future
Layne will microwave the popcorn.	past	present	(future)
Jackie planted the garden.	(past)	present	future
Marco will arrange the flowers.	past	present	(future)
The soup boiled over onto the stove.	(past)	present	future
Chris will lounge in the hammock.	past	present	(future)
The saw cut through the tree limb.	(past)	present	future
The driver backed into the parking space.	(past)	present	future
Hailey slapped the card onto the table.	(past)	present	future
The chef prepares dinner.	past	(present)	future
The jellyfish will float on the waves.	past	present	(future)
Meg pesters her sister.	past	(present)	future
Ernie will bait the hook.	past	present	(future)
Nell will chew the strawberry bubble gum.	past	present	(future)
Maddie and Deb manipulate the controls.	past	(present)	future
Rich searched for frogs and crayfish in the pond.	(past)	present	future

Review Work
Underline the nouns with yellow.

Draft Book
Write two sentences for each verb tense.
Underline the verbs with blue. Label the sentences past, present, or future tense.

© Carson-Dellosa CD-4339 Grammar Rules! Grades 5–6 **27**

RW: Underline barrel, rainwater, Jamie, friend, Layne, popcorn, Jackie, garden, Marco, flowers, soup, stove, Chris, hammock, saw, limb, driver, space, Hailey, card, table, chef, dinner, jellyfish, waves, Meg, sister, Ernie, hook, Nell, bubble gum, Maddie, Deb, controls, Rich, frogs, crayfish, and pond with yellow.
DB: Answers will vary.

Page 28

Name ____________________

Regular Describers — adjectives

Adjectives are words that describe nouns. Adjectives tell what kind, how many, or which one. They can include number, color, size, shape, or other detail words.
examples: The **dirty** puppy needs a bath. The **public** library is closed today.
A sentence can have more than one adjective.
example: **Four, gray** bugs are in the **small** garden.

Circle the adjectives. Draw an arrow from each adjective to the noun it describes.

A (wood-handled) shovel leaned against the (old, red) wheelbarrow.
The (filthy) refrigerator needed to be scoured.
I have (mint) gum in my (top) drawer.
The (new purple) pen is leaking ink.
(Five colorful) birds swooped through the (warm) air.
A (tired) Pete found (muddy) footprints on the (clean) floor.
A (riderless) skateboard zoomed down the (steep) hill.
Alicia jumped into the (cool pool) water.
The (itchy) bumps were not (bug) bites.
The (glowing) coals were ready to cook the (raw) hamburger.
Grandma gave us (cherry) pie with (vanilla) ice cream.
An (uncooperative) child threw an (enormous) fit in the restaurant.

Review Work
Underline the simple predicates twice.

Draft Book
Write 10 sentences that have adjectives in them. Circle each adjective. Draw an arrow from the adjective to the noun it describes.

28 CD-4339 Grammar Rules! Grades 5–6 © Carson-Dellosa

RW: Underline leaned, needed, have, is, swooped, found, zoomed, jumped, were, were, gave, and threw twice. DB: Answers will vary.

Page 29

Name ____________________

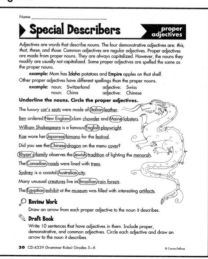

Other Describers — demonstrative and common adjectives

Adjectives are words that describe nouns. Adjectives tell what kind, how many, or which one. They can include number, color, size, shape, or other detail words. The four demonstrative adjectives that answer which one are: *this, that, these,* and *those.* Common adjectives are regular adjectives.

Circle the adjectives. Draw an arrow from each adjective to the noun it describes.

(Those scented) candles produce very (hot) wax.
(That four-year-old) child chatters constantly.
(This fuzzy) peach has a (bruised) spot.
(Those majestic) glaciers tower above (this cruise) ship.
(That dirty blue) sock has a (small) hole in the toe.
(This yellow) pencil has a (broken) point.
My (little) sister is in (that) class.
Barney wants (that chocolate) cupcake with (white) frosting.
Vera drew (that seaside) sketch with the (thunderous storm) clouds.
(These tiny black) seeds can grow (delicious white) radishes.
(Those glass) marbles belong to (that) boy.
(That black) camera takes (great) photographs.

Review Work
Write a *D* above each demonstrative adjective.

Draft Book
Write 10 sentences that have adjectives in them. Circle each adjective. Draw an arrow from the adjective to the noun it describes.

© Carson-Dellosa CD-4339 Grammar Rules! Grades 5–6 **29**

RW: Write a D above those, that, this, those, this, that, this, that, that, that, these, those, that, and that. DB: Answers will vary.

Page 30

Name ____________________

Special Describers — proper adjectives

Adjectives are words that describe nouns. The four demonstrative adjectives are: *this, that, these,* and *those.* Common adjectives are regular adjectives. Proper adjectives are made from proper nouns. They are always capitalized. However, the nouns they modify are usually not capitalized. Some proper adjectives are spelled the same as the proper nouns.
example: Mom has **Idaho** potatoes and **Empire** apples on that shelf.
Other proper adjectives have different spellings than the proper nouns.
example: noun: Switzerland adjective: Swiss
noun: China adjective: Chinese

Underline the nouns. Circle the proper adjectives.

The luxury car's seats were made of (Italian) leather.
Ben ordered (New England) clam chowder and (Maine) lobsters.
William Shakespeare is a famous (English) playwright.
Koe wore her (Japanese) kimono for the festival.
Did you see the (Chinese) dragon on the menu cover?
(Rhyan's) family observes the (Jewish) tradition of lighting the menorah.
The (Canadian) roads were lined with trees.
Sydney is a coastal (Australian) city.
Many unusual creatures live in (Brazilian) rain forests.
The (Egyptian) exhibit at the museum was filled with interesting artifacts.

Review Work
Draw an arrow from each proper adjective to the noun it describes.

Draft Book
Write 10 sentences that have adjectives in them. Include proper, demonstrative, and common adjectives. Circle each adjective and draw an arrow to the noun it describes.

30 CD-4339 Grammar Rules! Grades 5–6 © Carson-Dellosa

Answer Key

Page 30 (cont.)

RW: Draw arrows to leather, chowder, lobsters, playwright, kimono, dragon, family, tradition, roads, city, rain forests, and exhibit.
DB: Answers will vary.

Page 31

Name ____________________

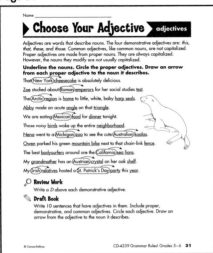

Choose Your Adjective — adjectives

Adjectives are words that describe nouns. The four demonstrative adjectives are: *this, that, these,* and *those.* Common adjectives, like common nouns, are not capitalized. Proper adjectives are made from proper nouns. They are always capitalized. However, the nouns they modify are not usually capitalized.

Underline the nouns. Circle the proper adjectives. Draw an arrow from each proper adjective to the noun it describes.

That (New York) cheesecake is absolutely delicious.
Zoe studied about (Roman) emperors for her social studies test.
The (Arctic) region is home to little, white, baby harp seals.
Abby made an acute angle on that triangle.
We are eating (Mexican) food for dinner tonight.
Those noisy birds woke up the entire neighborhood.
Nena went to a (Michigan) zoo to see the cute (Australian) koalas.
Owen parked his green mountain bike next to that chain-link fence.
The best bodysurfers around are the (California) sea lions.
My grandmother has an (Austrian) crystal on her oak shelf.
My (Irish) relatives hosted a (St. Patrick's Day) party this year.

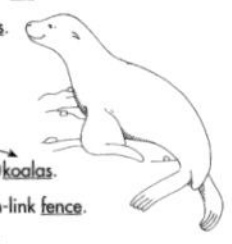

Review Work
Write a *D* above each demonstrative adjective.

Draft Book
Write 10 sentences that have adjectives in them. Include proper, demonstrative, and common adjectives. Circle each adjective. Draw an arrow from the adjective to the noun it describes.

© Carson-Dellosa — CD-4339 Grammar Rules! Grades 5–6 — 31

RW: Write a D above that, that, those, that, and this. DB: Answers will vary.

Page 32

Name ____________________

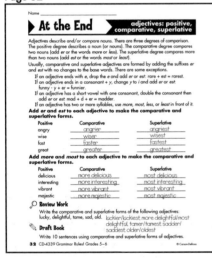

At the End — adjectives: positive, comparative, superlative

Adjectives describe and/or compare nouns. There are three degrees of comparison. The positive degree describes a noun (or nouns). The comparative degree compares two nouns (add *er* or the words *more* or *less*). The superlative degree compares more than two nouns (add *est* or the words *most* or *least*).
Usually, comparative and superlative adjectives are formed by adding the suffixes *er* and *est* with no changes to the base words. There are some exceptions.
If an adjective ends with *e*, drop the *e* and add *er* or *est*: rare + est = rarest.
If an adjective ends in a consonant + *y*, change *y* to *i* and add *er* or *est*: funny - y + er = funnier.
If an adjective has a short vowel with one consonant, double the consonant then add *er* or *est*: mad + d + er = madder.
If an adjective has two or more syllables, use *more, most, less,* or *least* in front of it.

Add *er* and *est* to each adjective to make the comparative and superlative forms.

Positive	Comparative	Superlative
angry	angrier	angriest
wise	wiser	wisest
fast	faster	fastest
great	greater	greatest

Add *more* and *most* to each adjective to make the comparative and superlative forms.

Positive	Comparative	Superlative
delicious	more delicious	most delicious
interesting	more interesting	most interesting
vibrant	more vibrant	most vibrant
majestic	more majestic	most majestic

Review Work
Write the comparative and superlative forms of the following adjectives: lucky, delightful, tame, sad, old. luckier/luckiest, more delightful/most delightful, tamer/tamest, sadder/saddest, older/oldest

Draft Book
Write 10 sentences using comparative and superlative forms of adjectives.

32 CD-4339 Grammar Rules! Grades 5–6 — © Carson-Dellosa

DB: Answers will vary.

Page 33

Name ____________________

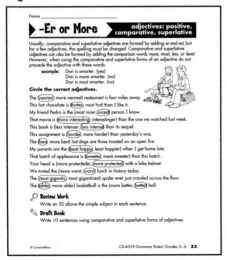

-Er or More — adjectives: positive, comparative, superlative

Usually, comparative and superlative adjectives are formed by adding *er* and *est*, but for a few adjectives, the spelling must be changed. Comparative and superlative adjectives can also be formed by adding the comparison words *more, most, less,* or *least.* However, when using the comparative and superlative forms of an adjective do not precede the adjective with these words.

example: Don is smarter. (yes)
Don is more smarter. (no)
Don is most smarter. (no)

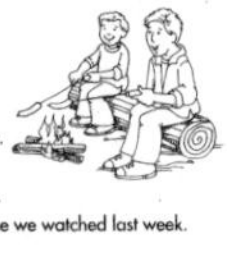

Circle the correct adjectives.

The (nearest) more nearest) restaurant is four miles away.
This hot chocolate is (hotter) most hot) than I like it.
My friend Pedro is the (most nicer, (nicest)) person I know.
That movie is ((more interesting), interestinger) than the one we watched last week.
This book is (less intenser, (less intense)) than its sequel.
This assignment is ((harder), more harder) than yesterday's was.
The ((best), more best) hot dogs are those toasted on an open fire.
My parents are the ((least happy), least happier) when I get home late.
That batch of applesauce is ((sweeter), more sweeter) than this batch.
Your head is (more protecteder, (more protected)) with a bike helmet.
We tasted the (more worst, (worst)) lunch in history today.
The ((most gigantic), most giganticest) spider ever just crawled across the floor.
The ((older), more older) basketball is the (more better, (better)) ball.

Review Work
Write an *SS* above the simple subject in each sentence.

Draft Book
Write 10 sentences using comparative and superlative forms of adjectives.

© Carson-Dellosa — CD-4339 Grammar Rules! Grades 5–6 — 33

Page 33 (cont.)

RW: Write an SS above restaurant, chocolate, Pedro, movie, book, assignment, hot dogs, parents, batch, head, we, spider, and basketball. DB: Answers will vary.

Page 34

Name ____________________

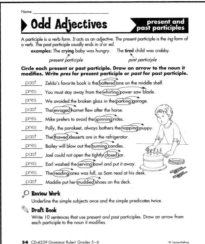

Odd Adjectives — present and past participles

A participle is a verb form. It acts as an adjective. The present participle is the *ing* form of a verb. The past participle usually ends in *d* or *ed.*
examples: The **crying** baby was hungry. The **tired** child was crabby.
present participle — past participle

Circle each present or past participle. Draw an arrow to the noun it modifies. Write *pres* for present participle or *past* for past participle.

past — Zelda's favorite book is the (battered) one on the middle shelf.
pres — You must stay away from the (whirling) power saw blade.
pres — We avoided the broken glass in the (parking) garage.
past — The (enraged) hornet flew after the horse.
pres — Mike prefers to avoid the (spinning) rides.
pres — Polly, the parakeet, always bothers the (napping) puppy.
past — The (thawed) desserts are in the refrigerator.
pres — Bailey will blow out the (burning) candles.
past — Joel could not open the tightly (closed) jar.
pres — Earl washed the (serving) bowl and put it away.
pres — The (reading) area was full, so Sam read at his desk.
past — Maddie put her (muddied) shoes on the deck.

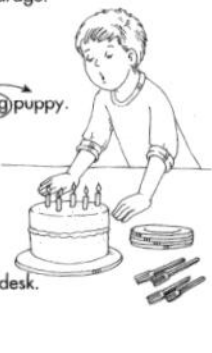

Review Work
Underline the simple subjects once and the simple predicates twice.

Draft Book
Write 10 sentences that use present and past participles. Draw an arrow from each participle to the noun it modifies.

34 CD-4339 Grammar Rules! Grades 5–6 — © Carson-Dellosa

RW: Underline book, you, we, hornet, Mike, Polly, desserts, Bailey, Joel, Earl, area, and Maddie once. Underline is, stay, avoided, flew, prefers, bothers, are, blow, open, washed, was, and put twice.
DB: Answers will vary.

Page 35

Name ____________________

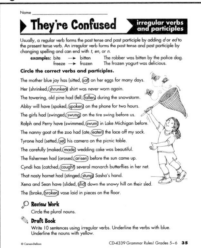

They're Confused — irregular verbs and participles

Usually, a regular verb forms the past tense and past participle by adding *d* or *ed* to the present tense verb. An irregular verb forms the past tense and past participle by changing spelling and can end with *t, en,* or *n.*
examples: bite → bitten — The robber was bitten by the police dog.
freeze → frozen — The frozen yogurt was delicious.

Circle the correct verbs and participles.

The mother blue jay has (sitted, (sat)) on her eggs for many days.
Her (shrinked, (shrunken)) shirt was never worn again.
The towering, old pine had (fell, (fallen)) during the snowstorm.
Abby will have (spoked, (spoken)) on the phone for two hours.
The girls had (swinged, (swung)) on the tire swing before us.
Ralph and Perry have (swimmed, (swum)) in Lake Michigan before.
The nanny goat at the zoo had (ate, (eaten)) the lace off my sock.
Tyrone had (setted, (set)) his camera on the picnic table.
The carefully (maked, (made)) wedding cake was beautiful.
The fishermen had (arosed, (arisen)) before the sun came up.
Cyndi has (catched, (caught)) several monarch butterflies in her net.
That nasty hornet had (stinged, (stung)) Sasha's hand.
Xena and Sean have (slided, (slid)) down the snowy hill on their sled.
The (broke, (broken)) vase laid in pieces on the floor.

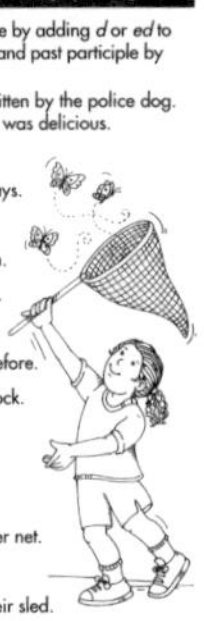

Review Work
Circle the plural nouns.

Draft Book
Write 10 sentences using irregular verbs. Underline the verbs with blue. Underline the nouns with yellow.

© Carson-Dellosa — CD-4339 Grammar Rules! Grades 5–6 — 35

RW: Circle eggs, days, hours, girls, butterflies, and pieces. DB: Answers will vary.

Page 36

Name ____________________

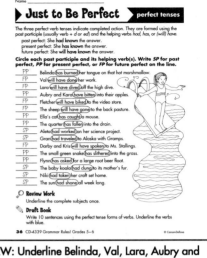

Just to Be Perfect — perfect tenses

The three perfect verb tenses indicate completed action. They are formed using the past participle (usually verb + *d* or *ed*) and the helping verbs *had, has,* or *(will) have.*
past perfect: She **had known** the answer.
present perfect: She **has known** the answer.
future perfect: She **will have known** the answer.

Circle each past participle and its helping verb(s). Write *SP* for past perfect, *PP* for present perfect, or *FP* for future perfect on the line.

PP — Belinda (has burned) her tongue on that hot marshmallow.
FP — Val (will have done) her work.
FP — Lara (will have dived) off the high dive.
PP — Aubry and Kara (have bitten) into their apples.
FP — Fletcher (will have biked) to the video store.
FP — The sheep (will have gone) to the back pasture.
PP — Ella's cat (has caught) a mouse.
PP — The quarter (has fallen) into the drain.
SP — Aleta (had worked) on her science project.
SP — Gran (had traveled) to Alaska with Gramps.
FP — Darby and Kris (will have spoken) to Ms. Stallings.
PP — The small green snake (has slithered) into the grass.
PP — Flynn (has asked) for a large root beer float.
SP — The baby koala (had clung) to its mother's fur.
SP — Niki (had taken) her craft set home.
SP — The sun (had shone) all week long.

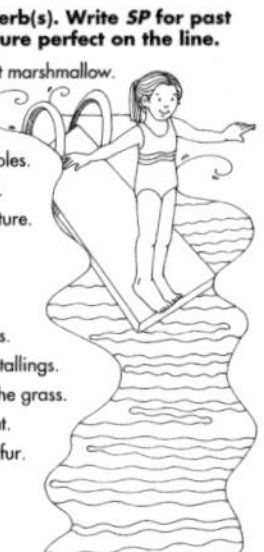

Review Work
Underline the complete subjects once.

Draft Book
Write 10 sentences using the perfect tense forms of verbs. Underline the verbs with blue.

36 CD-4339 Grammar Rules! Grades 5–6 — © Carson-Dellosa

RW: Underline Belinda, Val, Lara, Aubry and Kara, Fletcher, the sheep, Ella's cat, the quarter, Aleta, Gran, Darby and Kris, the small green snake, Flynn, the baby koala, Niki, and the sun once. DB: Answers will vary.

Page 37

Name ____________________

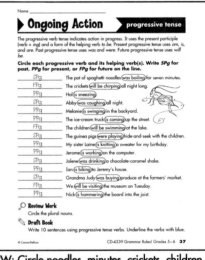

Ongoing Action — progressive tense

The progressive verb tense indicates action in progress. It uses the present participle (verb + *ing*) and a form of the helping verb *to be.* Present progressive tense uses *am, is,* and *are.* Past progressive tense uses *was* and *were.* Future progressive tense uses *will be.*

Circle each progressive verb and its helping verb(s). Write *SPg* for past, *PPg* for present, or *FPg* for future on the line.

SPg — The pot of spaghetti noodles (was boiling) for seven minutes.
FPg — The crickets (will be chirping) all night long.
PPg — Hal (is sneezing).
SPg — Abby (was coughing) all night.
PPg — Melanie (is swinging) in the backyard.
PPg — The ice-cream truck (is coming) up the street.
FPg — The children (will be swimming) at the lake.
SPg — The guinea pigs (were playing) hide-and-seek with the children.
PPg — My sister Laine (is knitting) a sweater for my birthday.
PPg — Jerome (is working) on the computer.
SPg — Jolene (was drinking) a chocolate-caramel shake.
PPg — Ian (is biking) to Jeremy's house.
SPg — Grandma Judy (was buying) produce at the farmers' market.
FPg — We (will be visiting) the museum on Tuesday.
PPg — Nick (is hammering) the board into the joist.

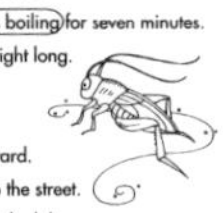

Review Work
Circle the plural nouns.

Draft Book
Write 10 sentences using progressive tense verbs. Underline the verbs with blue.

© Carson-Dellosa — CD-4339 Grammar Rules! Grades 5–6 — 37

RW: Circle noodles, minutes, crickets, children, guinea pigs, and children.
DB: Answers will vary.

Page 38

Name ____________________

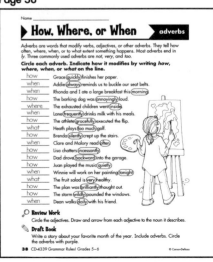

How, Where, or When — adverbs

Adverbs are words that modify verbs, adjectives, or other adverbs. They tell how often, where, when, or to what extent something happens. Most adverbs end in *ly.* Three commonly used adverbs are *not, very,* and *too.*

Circle each adverb. Indicate how it modifies by writing *how, where, when,* or *what* on the line.

how — Grace (quickly) finishes her paper.
when — Addie (always) reminds us to buckle our seat belts.
when — Rhonda and I ate a large breakfast this (morning).
how — The barking dog was (annoyingly) loud.
where — The exhausted children went (inside).
when — Lane (frequently) drinks milk with his meals.
how — The athlete (gracefully) executed the flip.
what — Heath plays (too much) golf.
how — Brenda (silently) crept up the stairs.
when — Clare and Malory read (often).
how — Lisa chatters (incessantly).
how — Dad drove (backward) into the garage.
how — Juan played the music (quietly).
when — Winnie will work on her painting (tonight).
what — The fruit salad is (very) healthy.
how — The plan was (brilliantly) thought out.
how — The storm (wildly) pounded the windows.
when — Dean walks (daily) with his friend.

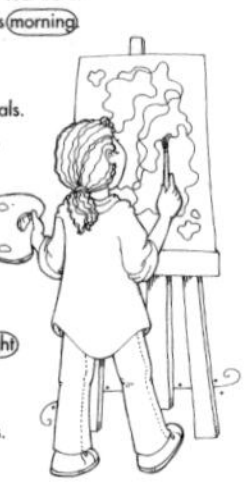

Review Work
Circle the adjectives. Draw and arrow from each adjective to the noun it describes.

Draft Book
Write a story about your favorite month of the year. Include adverbs. Circle the adverbs with purple.

38 CD-4339 Grammar Rules! Grades 5–6 — © Carson-Dellosa

Answer Key

Page 38 (cont.)
RW: Circle large, this, barking, exhausted, and fruit. Draw arrows to breakfast, morning, dog, children, and salad. DB: Answers will vary.

Page 39

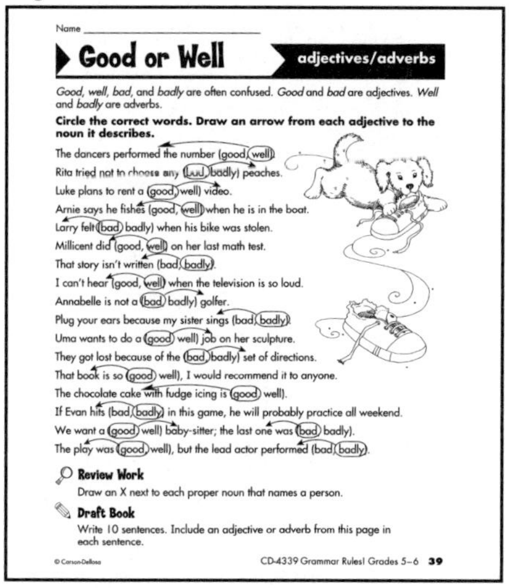

Name ____________

Good or Well — adjectives/adverbs

Good, well, bad, and *badly* are often confused. *Good* and *bad* are adjectives. *Well* and *badly* are adverbs.

Circle the correct words. Draw an arrow from each adjective to the noun it describes.

The dancers performed the number (good, well).
Rita tried not to choose any (bad, badly) peaches.
Luke plans to rent a (good, well) video.
Arnie says he fishes (good, well) when he is in the boat.
Larry felt (bad, badly) when his bike was stolen.
Millicent did (good, well) on her last math test.
That story isn't written (bad, badly).
I can't hear (good, well) when the television is so loud.
Annabelle is not a (bad, badly) golfer.
Plug your ears because my sister sings (bad, badly).
Uma wants to do a (good, well) job on her sculpture.
They got lost because of the (bad, badly) set of directions.
That book is so (good, well), I would recommend it to anyone.
The chocolate cake with fudge icing is (good, well).
If Evan hits (bad, badly) in this game, he will probably practice all weekend.
We want a (good, well) baby-sitter; the last one was (bad, badly).
The play was (good, well), but the lead actor performed (bad, badly).

Review Work
Draw an X next to each proper noun that names a person.

Draft Book
Write 10 sentences. Include an adjective or adverb from this page in each sentence.

© Carson-Dellosa CD-4339 Grammar Rules! Grades 5–6 39

RW: Draw an X next to Rita, Luke, Arnie, Larry, Millicent, Annabelle, Uma, and Evan.
DB: Answers will vary.

Page 40
Answers will vary.
RW: Underline they, he, she, she, and we with red. DB: Answers will vary.

Page 41

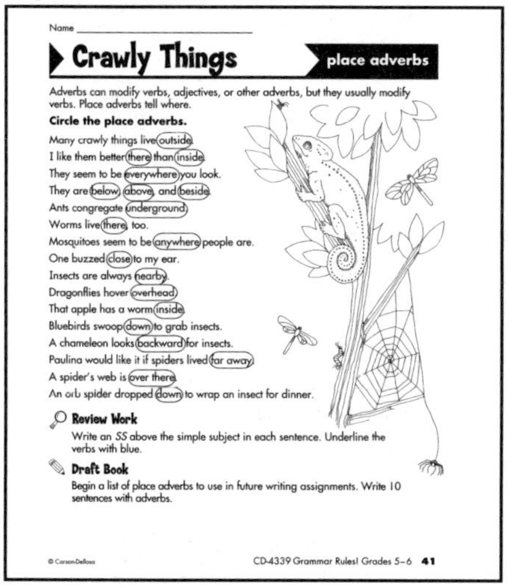

Name ____________

Crawly Things — place adverbs

Adverbs can modify verbs, adjectives, or other adverbs, but they usually modify verbs. Place adverbs tell where.

Circle the place adverbs.

Many crawly things live outside.
I like them better there than inside.
They seem to be everywhere you look.
They are below, above, and beside.
Ants congregate underground.
Worms live there, too.
Mosquitoes seem to be anywhere people are.
One buzzed close to my ear.
Insects are always nearby.
Dragonflies hover overhead.
That apple has a worm inside.
Bluebirds swoop down to grab insects.
A chameleon looks backward for insects.
Paulina would like it if spiders lived far away.
A spider's web is over there.
An orb spider dropped down to wrap an insect for dinner.

Review Work
Write an *SS* above the simple subject in each sentence. Underline the verbs with blue.

Draft Book
Begin a list of place adverbs to use in future writing assignments. Write 10 sentences with adverbs.

© Carson-Dellosa CD-4339 Grammar Rules! Grades 5–6 41

RW: Write an SS above things, I, they, they, ants, worms, mosquitoes, one, insects, dragonflies, apple, bluebirds, chameleon, Paulina, web, and spider. Underline live, like, seem, are, congregate, live, seem, buzzed, are, hover, has, swoop, looks, would like, is, and dropped with blue.
DB: Answers will vary.

Page 42

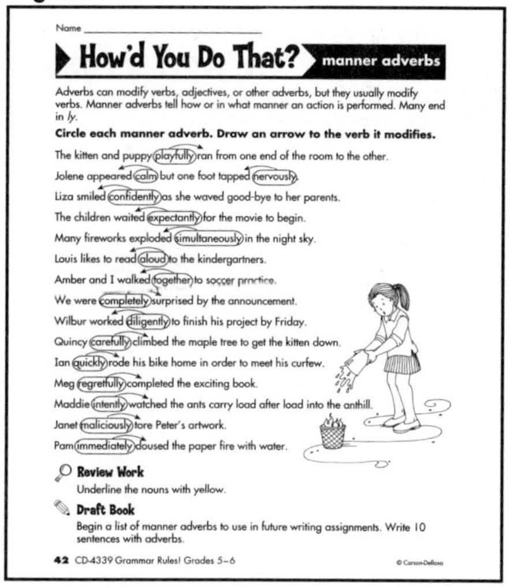

Name ____________

How'd You Do That? — manner adverbs

Adverbs can modify verbs, adjectives, or other adverbs, but they usually modify verbs. Manner adverbs tell how or in what manner an action is performed. Many end in *ly*.

Circle each manner adverb. Draw an arrow to the verb it modifies.

The kitten and puppy playfully ran from one end of the room to the other.
Jolene appeared calm but one foot tapped nervously.
Liza smiled confidently as she waved good-bye to her parents.
The children waited expectantly for the movie to begin.
Many fireworks exploded simultaneously in the night sky.
Louis likes to read aloud to the kindergartners.
Amber and I walked together to soccer practice.
We were completely surprised by the announcement.
Wilbur worked diligently to finish his project by Friday.
Quincy carefully climbed the maple tree to get the kitten down.
Ian quickly rode his bike home in order to meet his curfew.
Meg regretfully completed the exciting book.
Maddie intently watched the ants carry load after load into the anthill.
Janet maliciously tore Peter's artwork.
Pam immediately doused the paper fire with water.

Review Work
Underline the nouns with yellow.

Draft Book
Begin a list of manner adverbs to use in future writing assignments. Write 10 sentences with adverbs.

42 CD-4339 Grammar Rules! Grades 5–6 © Carson-Dellosa

RW: Underline kitten, puppy, end, room, other, Jolene, foot, Liza, parents, children, movie, fireworks, sky, Louis, kindergartners, Amber, practice, announcement, Wilbur, project, Friday, Quincy, tree, kitten, Ian, bike, curfew, Meg, book, Maddie, ants, load, load, anthill, Janet, artwork, Pam, fire, and water with yellow.
DB: Answers will vary.

Page 43

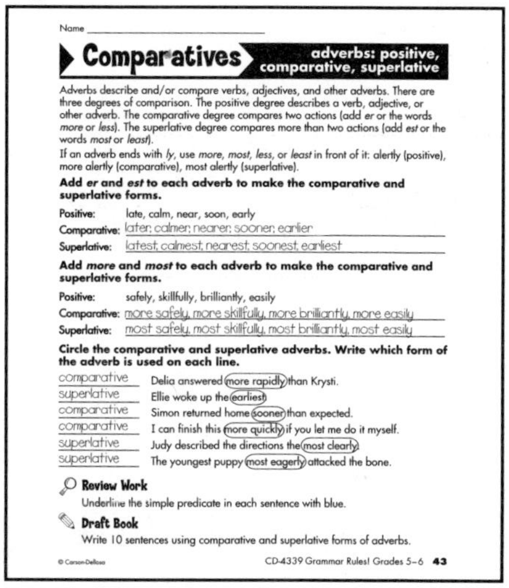

Name ____________

Comparatives — adverbs: positive, comparative, superlative

Adverbs describe and/or compare verbs, adjectives, and other adverbs. There are three degrees of comparison. The positive degree describes a verb, adjective, or other adverb. The comparative degree compares two actions (add *er* or the words *more* or *less*). The superlative degree compares more than two actions (add *est* or the words *most* or *least*).
If an adverb ends with *ly*, use *more, most, less,* or *least* in front of it: alertly (positive), more alertly (comparative), most alertly (superlative).

Add *er* and *est* to each adverb to make the comparative and superlative forms.

Positive: late, calm, near, soon, early
Comparative: later, calmer, nearer, sooner, earlier
Superlative: latest, calmest, nearest, soonest, earliest

Add *more* and *most* to each adverb to make the comparative and superlative forms.

Positive: safely, skillfully, brilliantly, easily
Comparative: more safely, more skillfully, more brilliantly, more easily
Superlative: most safely, most skillfully, most brilliantly, most easily

Circle the comparative and superlative adverbs. Write which form of the adverb is used on each line.

comparative — Delia answered more rapidly than Krysti.
superlative — Ellie woke up the earliest.
comparative — Simon returned home sooner than expected.
comparative — I can finish this more quickly if you let me do it myself.
superlative — Judy described the directions the most clearly.
superlative — The youngest puppy most eagerly attacked the bone.

Review Work
Underline the simple predicate in each sentence with blue.

Draft Book
Write 10 sentences using comparative and superlative forms of adverbs.

© Carson-Dellosa CD-4339 Grammar Rules! Grades 5–6 43

RW: Underline answered, woke, returned, finish, described, and attacked with blue.
DB: Answers will vary.

Page 44

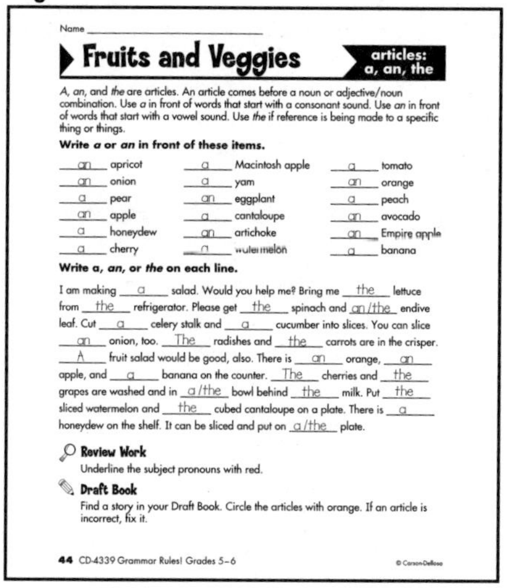

Name ____________

Fruits and Veggies — articles: a, an, the

A, an, and *the* are articles. An article comes before a noun or adjective/noun combination. Use *a* in front of words that start with a consonant sound. Use *an* in front of words that start with a vowel sound. Use *the* if reference is being made to a specific thing or things.

Write *a* or *an* in front of these items.

an apricot	a Macintosh apple	a tomato
an onion	a yam	an orange
a pear	an eggplant	a peach
an apple	a cantaloupe	an avocado
a honeydew	an artichoke	an Empire apple
a cherry	a watermelon	a banana

Write *a, an,* or *the* on each line.

I am making a salad. Would you help me? Bring me the lettuce from the refrigerator. Please get the spinach and an/the endive leaf. Cut a celery stalk and a cucumber into slices. You can slice an onion, too. The radishes and the carrots are in the crisper. A fruit salad would be good, also. There is an orange, an apple, and a banana on the counter. The cherries and the grapes are washed and in a/the bowl behind the milk. Put the sliced watermelon and the cubed cantaloupe on a plate. There is a honeydew on the shelf. It can be sliced and put on a/the plate.

Review Work
Underline the subject pronouns with red.

Draft Book
Find a story in your Draft Book. Circle the articles with orange. If an article is incorrect, fix it.

44 CD-4339 Grammar Rules! Grades 5–6 © Carson-Dellosa

RW: Underline I, you, you, and it with red.
DB: Answers will vary.

Page 45

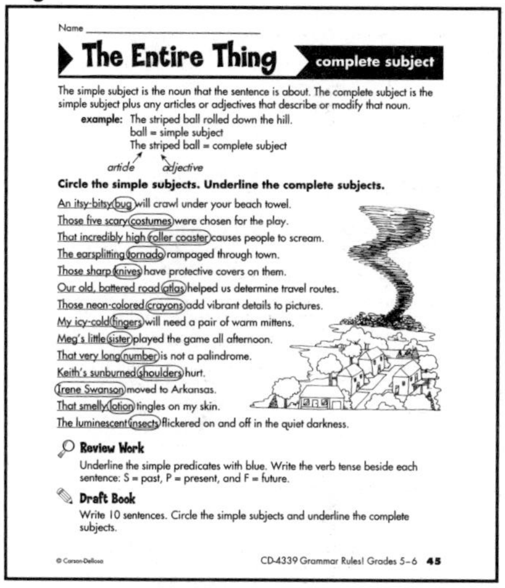

Name ____________

The Entire Thing — complete subject

The simple subject is the noun that the sentence is about. The complete subject is the simple subject plus any articles or adjectives that describe or modify that noun.

example: The striped ball rolled down the hill.
ball = simple subject
The striped ball = complete subject
article, adjective

Circle the simple subjects. Underline the complete subjects.

An itsy-bitsy bug will crawl under your beach towel.
Those five scary costumes were chosen for the play.
That incredibly high roller coaster causes people to scream.
The earsplitting tornado rampaged through town.
Those sharp knives have protective covers on them.
Our old, battered road atlas helped us determine travel routes.
Those neon-colored crayons add vibrant details to pictures.
My icy-cold fingers will need a pair of warm mittens.
Meg's little sister played the game all afternoon.
That very long number is not a palindrome.
Keith's sunburned shoulders hurt.
Irene Swanson moved to Arkansas.
That smelly lotion tingles on my skin.
The luminescent insects flickered on and off in the quiet darkness.

Review Work
Underline the simple predicates with blue. Write the verb tense beside each sentence: S = past, P = present, and F = future.

Draft Book
Write 10 sentences. Circle the simple subjects and underline the complete subjects.

© Carson-Dellosa CD-4339 Grammar Rules! Grades 5–6 45

RW: Underline crawl, chosen, causes, rampaged, have, helped, add, need, played, is, hurt, moved, tingles, and flickered with blue.
1. F 2. F 3. P 4. S 5. P 6. S 7. P 8. F 9. S 10. P 11. P 12. S 13. P 14. S
DB: Answers will vary.

Page 46

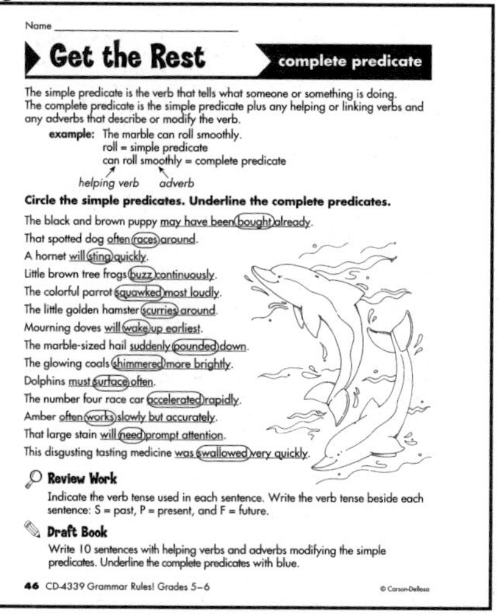

Name ____________

Get the Rest — complete predicate

The simple predicate is the verb that tells what someone or something is doing. The complete predicate is the simple predicate plus any helping or linking verbs and any adverbs that describe or modify the verb.

example: The marble can roll smoothly.
roll = simple predicate
can roll smoothly = complete predicate
helping verb, adverb

Circle the simple predicates. Underline the complete predicates.

The black and brown puppy may have been bought already.
That spotted dog often races around.
A hornet will sting quickly.
Little brown tree frogs buzz continuously.
The colorful parrot squawked most loudly.
The little golden hamster scurries around.
Mourning doves will wake up earliest.
The marble-sized hail suddenly pounded down.
The glowing coals shimmered more brightly.
Dolphins must surface often.
The number four race car accelerated rapidly.
Amber often works slowly but accurately.
That large stain will need prompt attention.
This disgusting tasting medicine was swallowed very quickly.

Review Work
Indicate the verb tense used in each sentence. Write the verb tense beside each sentence: S = past, P = present, and F = future.

Draft Book
Write 10 sentences with helping verbs and adverbs modifying the simple predicates. Underline the complete predicates with blue.

46 CD-4339 Grammar Rules! Grades 5–6 © Carson-Dellosa

Page 46 (cont.)

RW: 1. S 2. P 3. F 4. P 5. S 6. P 7. F 8. S
9. S 10. P 11. S 12. P 13. F 14. S
DB: Answers will vary.

Page 47

The Whole Predicate — complete predicate

The complete predicate is the simple predicate plus any helping or linking verbs, any adverbs, and any other words that modify the verb. If the words are not part of the complete subject, they are included in the complete predicate.

example: Bob will bike to the beach.

The big, red apple fell to the ground.

Sally played with her brother.

Circle the simple predicates. Underline the complete predicates.

Violet was responsible for feeding the fish.
The glass of soda spilled across the table.
The sun sparkles blindingly off the snow.
The enormous block tower toppled.
Sleepy children awoke to frosted windows.
The winter snowman melted away to nothing.
Madalen slept with one arm around her teddy bear.
The price of stamps will rise at the end of June.
The glowing space heater pumps out waves of comforting heat.
The dinner-plate-sized blooms popped open overnight.
The striped beach ball drifted just out of reach.
Alicia surfaced coughing and sputtering.
This suction cup will stick securely to the window.

Review Work
Indicate the verb tense used in each sentence. Write the verb tense beside each sentence: S = past, P = present, and F = future.

Draft Book
Write 10 sentences. Underline the complete predicates with blue.

CD-4339 Grammar Rules! Grades 5–6 **47**

RW: 1. S 2. S 3. P 4. S 5. S 6. S 7. S 8. F
9. P 10. S 11. S 12. S 13. F
DB: Answers will vary.

Page 48

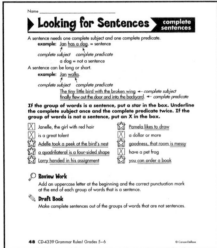

Looking for Sentences — complete sentences

A sentence needs one complete subject and one complete predicate.

example: Jan has a dog. = sentence

complete subject   complete predicate

a dog = not a sentence

A sentence can be long or short.

example: Jan walks.

complete subject   complete predicate

The tiny bird with the broken wing ← complete subject
finally flew out the door and into the backyard. ← complete predicate

If the group of words is a sentence, put a star in the box. Underline the complete subject once and the complete predicate twice. If the group of words is not a sentence, put an X in the box.

[X] Janelle, the girl with red hair   [X] Pamela likes to draw
[X] is a great talent   [X] a dollar or more
[★] Adelle took a peek at the bird's nest   [X] goodness, that room is messy
[★] a quadrilateral is a four-sided shape   [X] have a pet frog
[★] Larry handed in his assignment   [X] you can order a book

Review Work
Add an uppercase letter at the beginning and the correct punctuation mark at the end of each group of words that is a sentence.

Draft Book
Make complete sentences out of the groups of words that are not sentences.

48 CD-4339 Grammar Rules! Grades 5–6

RW: Add correct beginning uppercase letter and ending punctuation to each sentence.
DB: Answers will vary.

Page 49
Answers will vary.

Page 50

Predicate Nouns — linking verbs and predicate nouns

A linking verb does not show action. It links or joins something in the predicate to the subject of the sentence. It does not have an action verb after it. A predicate noun is a noun that follows the linking verb and tells something about the subject.

Underline the linking verbs. Circle the predicate nouns. Draw an arrow from each predicate noun to the simple subject it tells more about.

The zebra mussel is a bivalve originally from Europe.
That girl in the third row was my sister.
Mrs. Stamey is a fifth-grade teacher.
I am a good student.
A solar calculator is a great math tool.
Jupiter is a massive ball of gas.
Venus is the second planet from the sun.
The first-chair trombone player is Marcus Bolan.
Our sun is actually a star.
That lumpy, dark green stone is raw jade.
This blue, white, and green yarn will be an afghan someday.
Those ladies are the star surgeons tonight.
That very large spider appears to be a tarantula.
Acrophobia is the fear of heights.

Review Work
Circle the adverbs with purple.

Draft Book
Write 10 sentences that use linking verbs and predicate nouns. Draw an arrow from each predicate noun to the subject it tells more about.

50 CD-4339 Grammar Rules! Grades 5–6

RW: Circle originally, actually, someday, and tonight with purple. DB: Answers will vary.

Page 51

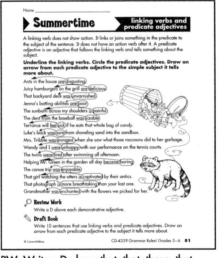

Summertime — linking verbs and predicate adjectives

A linking verb does not show action. It links or joins something in the predicate to the subject of the sentence. It does not have an action verb after it. A predicate adjective is an adjective that follows the linking verb and tells something about the subject.

Underline the linking verbs. Circle the predicate adjectives. Draw an arrow from each predicate adjective to the simple subject it tells more about.

Ants in the house are disgusting.
Juicy hamburgers on the grill are delicious.
That backyard deck was unvarnished.
Jenna's batting abilities are poor.
The sunburn across my shoulders is painful.
The dent from the baseball was sizable.
Terrance will feel sick if he eats that whole bag of candy.
Luke's back was sore from shoveling sand into the sandbox.
Mrs. Tribble was enraged when she saw what those raccoons did to her garbage.
Wendy and I were unhappy with our performance on the tennis courts.
The twins were tired after swimming all afternoon.
Helping Mr. Green in the garden all day became boring.
The canoe trip was enjoyable.
That girl watching the otters is captivated by their antics.
That photograph is more breathtaking than your last one.
Grandmother was enchanted with the flowers we picked for her.

Review Work
Write a D above each demonstrative adjective.

Draft Book
Write 10 sentences that use linking verbs and predicate adjectives. Draw an arrow from each predicate adjective to the subject it tells more about.

CD-4339 Grammar Rules! Grades 5–6 **51**

RW: Write a D above that, that, those, that, and that. DB: Answers will vary.

Page 52

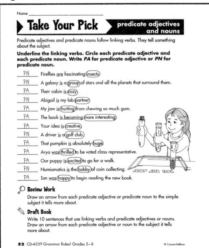

Take Your Pick — predicate adjectives and nouns

Predicate adjectives and predicate nouns follow linking verbs. They tell something about the subject.

Underline the linking verbs. Circle each predicate adjective and each predicate noun. Write PA for predicate adjective or PN for predicate noun.

PN Fireflies are fascinating insects.
PN A galaxy is a group of stars and all the planets that surround them.
PA Their cabin is cozy.
PN Abigail is my lab partner.
PA My jaw is hurting from chewing so much gum.
PA The book is becoming more interesting.
PA Your idea is creative.
PN A driver is a golf club.
PA That pumpkin is absolutely huge.
PA Arya was thrilled to be voted class representative.
PA Our puppy is excited to go for a walk.
PN Numismatics is the hobby of coin collecting.
PA Ian was happy to begin reading the new book.

Review Work
Draw an arrow from each predicate adjective or predicate noun to the simple subject it tells more about.

Draft Book
Write 10 sentences that use linking verbs and predicate adjectives or nouns. Draw an arrow from each predicate adjective or noun to the subject it tells more about.

52 CD-4339 Grammar Rules! Grades 5–6

RW: Draw arrows to fireflies, galaxy, cabin, Abigail, jaw, book, idea, driver, pumpkin, Arya, puppy, numismatics, and Ian.
DB: Answers will vary.

Page 53

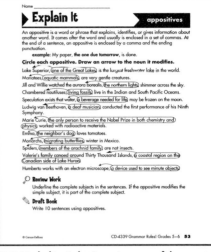

Explain It — appositives

An appositive is a word or phrase that explains, identifies, or gives information about another word. It comes after the word and usually is enclosed in a set of commas. At the end of a sentence, an appositive is enclosed by a comma and the ending punctuation.

example: My paper, the one due tomorrow, is done.

Circle each appositive. Draw an arrow to the noun it modifies.

Lake Superior, one of the Great Lakes, is the largest freshwater lake in the world.
Manatees, aquatic mammals, are very gentle creatures.
Jill and Willie watched the aurora borealis, the northern lights, shimmer across the sky.
Chambered nautiluses, living fossils, live in the Indian and South Pacific Oceans.
Speculation exists that water, a beverage needed for life, may be frozen on the moon.
Ludwig van Beethoven, a deaf musician, conducted the first performance of his Ninth Symphony.
Marie Curie, the only person to receive the Nobel Prize in both chemistry and physics, worked with radioactive materials.
Emma, the neighbor's dog, loves tomatoes.
Monarchs, migrating butterflies, winter in Mexico.
Spiders, members of the arachnid family, are not insects.
Valerie's family canoed around Thirty Thousand Islands, a coastal region on the Canadian side of Lake Huron.
Humberto works with an electron microscope, a device used to see minute objects.

Review Work
Underline the complete subjects in the sentences. If the appositive modifies the simple subject, it is part of the complete subject.

Draft Book
Write 10 sentences using appositives.

CD-4339 Grammar Rules! Grades 5–6 **53**

RW: Underline Lake Superior, one of the great lakes; manatees, aquatic mammals; Jill and Willie; chambered nautiluses, living fossils; speculation exists that water, a beverage needed for life; Ludwig van Beethoven, a deaf musician; Marie Curie, the only person to receive the Nobel Prize in both chemistry and physics; Emma, the neighbor's dog; monarchs, migrating butterflies; spiders, members of the arachnid family; Valerie's family; and Humberto. DB: Answers will vary.

Page 54

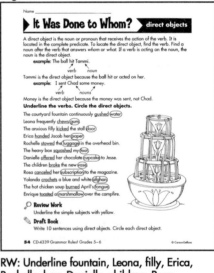

It Was Done to Whom? — direct objects

A direct object is the noun or pronoun that receives the action of the verb. It is located in the complete predicate. To locate the direct object, find the verb. Find a noun after the verb that answers whom or what. If a verb is acting on the noun, the noun is the direct object.

example: The ball hit Tammi.
verb   noun

Tammi is the direct object because the ball hit or acted on her.

example: I sent Chad some money.
verb   nouns

Money is the direct object because the money was sent, not Chad.

Underline the verbs. Circle the direct objects.

The courtyard fountain continuously gushed water.
Leona frequently chews gum.
The anxious filly kicked the stall door.
Erica handed Jacob her paper.
Rochelle stowed the luggage in the overhead bin.
The heavy box squashed my foot.
Danielle offered her chocolate cupcake to Jesse.
The children broke the new vase.
Rosa canceled her subscription to the magazine.
Yolanda crochets a blue and white afghan.
The hot chicken soup burned April's tongue.
Enrique toasted a marshmallow over the campfire.

Review Work
Underline the simple subjects with yellow.

Draft Book
Write 10 sentences using direct objects. Circle each direct object.

54 CD-4339 Grammar Rules! Grades 5–6

RW: Underline fountain, Leona, filly, Erica, Rochelle, box, Danielle, children, Rosa, Yolanda, soup, and Enrique with yellow.
DB: Answers will vary.

Answer Key

Page 55

Name ____________________

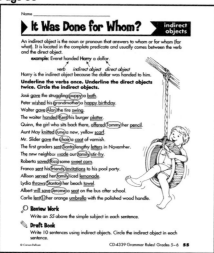

It Was Done for Whom? — indirect objects

An indirect object is the noun or pronoun that answers to whom or for whom (for what). It is located in the complete predicate and usually comes between the verb and the direct object.

example: Everet handed **Harry** a dollar.
verb *indirect object* *direct object*

Harry is the indirect object because the dollar was handed to him.

Underline the verbs once. Underline the direct objects twice. Circle the indirect objects.

José gave the struggling puppy a bath.
Peter wished his grandmother a happy birthday.
Walter gave Alan the tire swing.
The waiter handed Ken his burger platter.
Quinn, the girl who sits back there, offered Tommy her pencil.
Aunt May knitted June a new, yellow scarf.
Mr. Slider gave the chair a coat of varnish.
The first graders sent Santa lengthy letters in November.
The new neighbor made our family stir-fry.
Roberta saved Rico some sweet corn.
Franco sent his friends invitations to his pool party.
Allison served her family iced lemonade.
Lydia throws Stanton her beach towel.
Albert will save Jerome a seat on the bus after school.
Carlie lent Li her orange umbrella with the polished wood handle.

Review Work
Write an *SS* above the simple subject in each sentence.

Draft Book
Write 10 sentences using indirect objects. Circle the indirect object in each sentence.

© Carson-Dellosa CD-4339 Grammar Rules! Grades 5–6 **55**

RW: Write an SS above José, Peter, Walter, waiter, Quinn, Aunt May, Mr. Slider, first graders, neighbor, Roberta, Franco, Allison, Lydia, Albert, and Carlie.
DB: Answers will vary.

Page 56

Answers will vary.

Page 57

Name ____________________

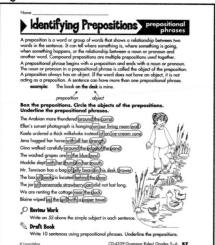

Identifying Prepositions — prepositional phrases

A preposition is a word or group of words that shows a relationship between two words in the sentence. It can tell where something is, where something is going, when something happens, or the relationship between a noun or pronoun and another word. Compound prepositions are multiple prepositions used together.

A prepositional phrase begins with a preposition and ends with a noun or pronoun. The noun or pronoun in a prepositional phrase is called the object of the preposition. A preposition always has an object. If the word does not have an object, it is not acting as a preposition. A sentence can have more than one prepositional phrase.

example: The book **on the desk** is mine.
preposition *object*

Box the prepositions. Circle the objects of the prepositions. Underline the prepositional phrases.

The Arabian mare thundered around the corral.
Ellen's sunset photograph is hanging on our living room wall.
Kaela ordered a thick milkshake instead of an ice-cream cone.
Jena hugged her horse with all her strength.
Gina walked carefully around the edge of the pond.
The washed grapes are in the blue bowl.
Maddie slept with her thumb in her mouth.
Mr. Tennison has a bag of jelly beans in his desk drawer.
The box of books is located behind the door.
The jar of homemade strawberry jam did not last long.
We are renting the cottage near the dock.
Blaine wiped up the spill with a paper towel.

Review Work
Write an *SS* above the simple subject in each sentence.

Draft Book
Write 10 sentences using prepositional phrases. Underline the prepositions.

© Carson-Dellosa CD-4339 Grammar Rules! Grades 5–6 **57**

RW: Write an SS above mare, photograph, Kaela, Jena, Gina, grapes, Maddie, Mr. Tennison, box, jar, we, and Blaine.
DB: Answers will vary.

Page 58

Name ____________________

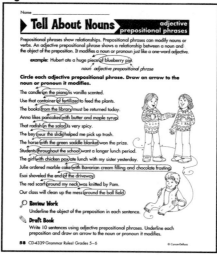

Tell About Nouns — adjective prepositional phrases

Prepositional phrases show relationships. Prepositional phrases can modify nouns or verbs. An adjective prepositional phrase shows a relationship between a noun and the object of the preposition. It modifies a noun or pronoun just like a one-word adjective.

example: Hubert ate a huge piece of blueberry pie.
noun *adjective prepositional phrase*

Circle each adjective prepositional phrase. Draw an arrow to the noun or pronoun it modifies.

The candle on the piano is vanilla scented.
Use that container of fertilizer to feed the plants.
The books from the library must be returned today.
Anna likes pancakes with butter and maple syrup.
That radish in the salad is very spicy.
The boy near the slide helped me pick up trash.
The horse with the green saddle blanket won the prize.
Students throughout the school want a longer lunch period.
The girl with chicken pox ate lunch with my sister yesterday.
Julie ordered marble cake with Bavarian cream filling and chocolate frosting.
Esai shoveled the end of the driveway.
The red scarf around my neck was knitted by Pam.
Our class will clean up the mess around the ball field.

Review Work
Underline the object of the preposition in each sentence.

Draft Book
Write 10 sentences using adjective prepositional phrases. Underline each preposition and draw an arrow to the noun or pronoun it modifies.

58 CD-4339 Grammar Rules! Grades 5–6 © Carson-Dellosa

RW: Underline piano, fertilizer, library, butter, maple syrup, salad, slide, blanket, filling, frosting, school, chicken pox, driveway, neck, and field. DB: Answers will vary.

Page 59

Name ____________________

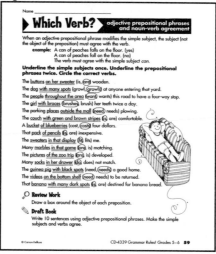

Which Verb? — adjective prepositional phrases and noun-verb agreement

When an adjective prepositional phrase modifies the simple subject, the subject (not the object of the preposition) must agree with the verb.

example: A can of peaches falls on the floor. (yes)
A can of peaches fall on the floor. (no)
The verb must agree with the simple subject *can*.

Underline the simple subjects once. Underline the prepositional phrases twice. Circle the correct verbs.

The buttons on her sweater (is, are) wooden.
The dog with many spots (growl, growls) at anyone entering that yard.
The people throughout the area (want, wants) this road to have a four-way stop.
The girl with braces (brushes, brush) her teeth twice a day.
The parking places outside the mall (need, needs) plowing.
The couch with green and brown stripes (is, are) comfortable.
A bucket of blueberries (cost, costs) four dollars.
That pack of pencils (is, are) inexpensive.
The sweaters in that display (fit, fits) me.
Many marbles in that game (are, is) matching.
The pictures of the zoo trip (are, is) developed.
Many socks in her drawer (do, does) not match.
The guinea pig with black spots (need, needs) a good home.
The videos on the bottom shelf (need, needs) to be returned.
That banana with many dark spots (is, are) destined for banana bread.

Review Work
Draw a box around the object of each preposition.

Draft Book
Write 10 sentences using adjective prepositional phrases. Make the simple subjects and verbs agree.

© Carson-Dellosa CD-4339 Grammar Rules! Grades 5–6 **59**

RW: Draw a box around sweater, spots, area, braces, mall, stripes, blueberies, pencils, display, game, trip, drawer, spots, shelf, and spots. DB: Answers will vary.

Page 60

Name ____________________

Tell About Verbs — adverb prepositional phrases

Prepositional phrases show relationships. Prepositional phrases can modify nouns or verbs. An adverb prepositional phrase modifies the verb. It tells how, where, when, or to what extent something happens just like a one-word adverb.

Underline each adverb prepositional phrase. Tell how it modifies the verb by writing *how, where, when,* or *what* on the line.

where — The trip photos are in the album.
where — David and Walter walked to the store.
what — The pitcher played beyond his average performance.
when — During yesterday's thunderstorm, the power went out.
where — The Girl Scout troop will sleep at Ms. Emma's house Friday night.
how — Without any complaining, Jade cleaned her room.
when — Olivia must be home before 7:00 p.m.
where — Geno will put that can into the recycle bin.
when — Their family vacations in June.
what — My dad ate ice cream and cookies until he was full.
how — Ned and I finished the project with assistance.
where — He went straight to his room.
where — Shelly found many monarch caterpillars on the milkweed plants.
when — We will visit our cousins over the holiday break.
when — On Saturday night, we saw the northern lights.
how — The neighborhood children had a snowball battle despite the freezing temperatures.

Review Work
Underline the simple subjects with yellow.

Draft Book
Write 10 sentences using a variety of adverb prepositional phrases.

60 CD-4339 Grammar Rules! Grades 5–6 © Carson-Dellosa

Page 60 (cont.)

RW: Underline photos, David, Walter, pitcher, power, troop, Jade, Olivia, Geno, family, dad, Ned, I, he, Shelly, we, we, and children with yellow. DB: Answers will vary.

Page 61

Name ____________________

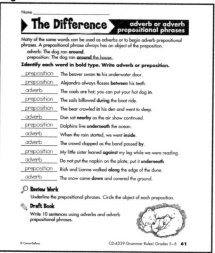

The Difference — adverb or adverb prepositional phrases

Many of the same words can be used as adverbs or to begin adverb prepositional phrases. A prepositional phrase always has an object of the preposition.
adverb: The dog ran **around**.
preposition: The dog ran **around** the house.

Identify each word in bold type. Write adverb or preposition.

preposition — The beaver swam **to** his underwater door.
preposition — Alejandro always flosses **between** his teeth.
adverb — The coals are hot; you can put your hot dog **in**.
preposition — The sails billowed **during** the boat ride.
preposition — The bear crawled **in** his den and went to sleep.
adverb — Dan sat **nearby** as the air show continued.
preposition — Dolphins live **underneath** the ocean.
adverb — When the rain started, we went **inside**.
adverb — The crowd clapped as the band passed **by**.
preposition — My little sister leaned **against** my leg while we were reading.
adverb — Do not put the napkin on the plate; put it **underneath**.
preposition — Rich and Lianne walked **along** the edge of the dune.
adverb — The snow came **down** and covered the ground.

Review Work
Underline the prepositional phrases. Circle the object of each preposition.

Draft Book
Write 10 sentences using adverbs and adverb prepositional phrases.

© Carson-Dellosa CD-4339 Grammar Rules! Grades 5–6 **61**

RW: Underline to his underwater door, between his teeth, during the boat ride, in his den, underneath the ocean, against my leg, and along the edge. Circle door, teeth, ride, den, ocean, leg, and edge. DB: Answers will vary.

Page 62

Name ____________________

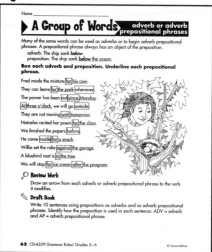

A Group of Words — adverb or adverb prepositional phrases

Many of the same words can be used as adverbs or to begin adverb prepositional phrases. A prepositional phrase always has an object of the preposition.
adverb: The ship sank **below**.
preposition: The ship sank **below** the ocean.

Box each adverb and preposition. Underline each prepositional phrase.

Fred made the mixture for his cow.
They can leave for the park whenever.
The power has been out since Monday.
At three o'clock, we will go outside.
They are not moving until tomorrow.
Natasha recited her poem for the class.
We finished the papers before.
He came inside for a snack.
Willie set the rake against the garage.
A bluebird nest is in the tree.
We will stop for ice cream after the program.

Review Work
Draw an arrow from each adverb or adverb prepositional phrase to the verb it modifies.

Draft Book
Write 10 sentences using prepositions as adverbs and as adverb prepositional phrases. Identify how the preposition is used in each sentence: ADV = adverb and AP = adverb prepositional phrase.

62 CD-4339 Grammar Rules! Grades 5–6 © Carson-Dellosa

RW: Write an SS above Fred, they, power, we, they, Natasha, we, he, Willie, bluebird, and we. DB: Answers will vary.

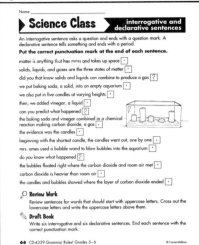

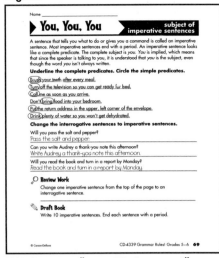

Page 63

Which Is Which? — adjective and adverb prepositional phrases

Prepositional phrases show relationships. Prepositional phrases can modify nouns or verbs. An adjective prepositional phrase modifies the noun. An adverb prepositional phrase modifies the verb.

Underline the prepositional phrases. Write *Adj* above each adjective prepositional phrase and *Adv* above each adverb prepositional phrase.

Dion put the night crawlers into the bucket. *(Adv)*
The bread in that bag is stale. *(Adj)*
The beekeeper delivered his bees to the fruit orchard. *(Adv)*
Talia reads a book in the morning. *(Adv)*
The cow from that farm is standing in the middle of the road. *(Adj)(Adv)*
The Milky Way is only one of many galaxies in the universe. *(Adj)(Adj)*
The crystal clips held her hair off her forehead. *(Adv)*
The box of chocolates melted in the trunk of the hot car. *(Adj)(Adv)*
Zach delivered the jar of homemade apricot jam. *(Adj)*
On Monday morning, Irma jogged five miles. *(Adv)*
Our team won the match despite playing on their field. *(Adv)*
Amber walked through the door of the gym. *(Adv)(Adj)*
Make a turn off this road at the next stop sign. *(Adv)(Adv)*
Renee swam across the pool to the deep end. *(Adv)(Adv)*

Review Work
Underline the verbs with blue.

Draft Book
Write 10 sentences using prepositional phrases. Write *Adj* above each adjective prepositional phrase and *Adv* above each adverb prepositional phrase.

CD-4339 Grammar Rules! Grades 5–6 **63**

RW: Underline put, is, delivered, reads, is standing, is, held, melted, delivered, jogged, won, walked, make, and swam. **DB: Answers will vary.**

Page 64

We Sound the Same — homophones

Homophones are words that sound alike but are spelled differently and have different meanings.

Write the correct homophone on each line.

its: possessive pronoun **it's:** contraction for it is
It's too late to go to the movie now.
The cottage has its own beach access.
Its top is scratched.
Erica believes it's too icy to drive to the library.

there: location word **their:** possessive pronoun **they're:** contraction for they are
Their house is on the cul-de-sac at the end of the street.
They're lots of fun to play games with.
Marcus and Cody went there for a cookout.
Riley really likes their llamas.
At the ice-cream shop, they're having a two-for-one special today.
Tamika will rest there before biking the last six miles.

your: possessive pronoun **you're:** contraction for you are
You're visiting the zoo with us this Wednesday.
Do you like your new hot tub?
I'm sorry you're not able to come to the cookout.

whose: interrogative pronoun **who's:** contraction for who is
Whose were you planning to paint first?
There is no name on this paper; whose is it?
The store wants to hire the student who's the most reliable.

Review Work
Underline the nouns with yellow.

Draft Book
Write three sentences for each homophone on this page.

64 CD-4339 Grammar Rules! Grades 5–6

RW: Underline movie, cottage, access, top, Erica, library, house, cul-de-sac, end, street, fun, games, Marcus, Cody, cookout, Riley, llamas, shop, special, Tamika, miles, zoo, Wednesday, hot tub, cookout, name, paper, store, and student. **DB: Answers will vary.**

Page 65
Answers will vary.

Page 66

Science Class — interrogative and declarative sentences

An interrogative sentence asks a question and ends with a question mark. A declarative sentence tells something and ends with a period.

Put the correct punctuation mark at the end of each sentence.

matter is anything that has mass and takes up space *(.)*
solids, liquids, and gases are the three states of matter *(.)*
did you that know solids and liquids can combine to produce a gas *(?)*
we put baking soda, a solid, into an empty aquarium *(.)*
we also put in five candles at varying heights *(.)*
then, we added vinegar, a liquid *(.)*
can you predict what happened *(?)*
the baking soda and vinegar combined in a chemical reaction making carbon dioxide, a gas *(.)*
the evidence was the candles *(.)*
beginning with the shortest candle, the candles went out, one by one *(.)*
mrs. ames used a bubble wand to blow bubbles into the aquarium *(.)*
do you know what happened *(?)*
the bubbles floated right where the carbon dioxide and room air met *(.)*
carbon dioxide is heavier than room air *(.)*
the candles and bubbles showed where the layer of carbon dioxide ended *(.)*

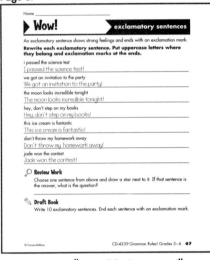

Review Work
Review sentences for words that should start with uppercase letters. Cross out the lowercase letters and write the uppercase letters above them.

Draft Book
Write six interrogative and six declarative sentences. End each sentence with the correct punctuation mark.

66 CD-4339 Grammar Rules! Grades 5–6

RW: Add uppercase letters where necessary. DB: Answers will vary.

Page 67

Wow! — exclamatory sentences

An exclamatory sentence shows strong feelings and ends with an exclamation mark.

Rewrite each exclamatory sentence. Put uppercase letters where they belong and exclamation marks at the ends.

i passed the science test
I passed the science test!
we got an invitation to the party
We got an invitation to the party!
the moon looks incredible tonight
The moon looks incredible tonight!
hey, don't step on my books
Hey, don't step on my books!
this ice cream is fantastic
This ice cream is fantastic!
don't throw my homework away
Don't throw my homework away!
jade won the contest
Jade won the contest!

Review Work
Choose one sentence from above and draw a star next to it. If that sentence is the answer, what is the question?

Draft Book
Write 10 exclamatory sentences. End each sentence with an exclamation mark.

CD-4339 Grammar Rules! Grades 5–6 **67**

RW: Answers will vary. DB: Answers will vary.

Page 68

With Feeling — imperative sentences

A sentence that tells you what to do or gives you a command is called an imperative sentence. Most imperative sentences end with periods. Occasionally, a command is given with great feeling. In this case, an exclamation mark is used. The same command can end with either a period or an exclamation mark depending on the situation.

example: Sit down. → Mom is asking you to sit down to dinner.
Sit down! → A small child is standing on a rocking chair, and it is about to tip over.

Read the situations. Put the correct punctuation at the end of each imperative sentence.

Stop that *(.)* A friend is tapping her pencil.
Stop that *(!)* Your brother is hitting your bruised shoulder.
Wash your hands *(!)* Someone touched poison ivy.
Wash your hands *(.)* It is dinnertime.
Put water on it *(!)* A fire started in the trash can.
Put water on it *(.)* The soil in the plant is beginning to dry.
Move *(.)* Your friend is lounging on the couch, and you would like to share.
Move *(!)* The bull has spotted your friend in his pasture and is racing toward her.
Get your dad *(.)* It is time for dinner.
Get your dad *(!)* The ladder fell down, and Mom is stuck on the roof.

Review Work
Give the situations for these two imperative sentences.
Run!
Run.

Draft Book
Write 10 imperative sentences. Begin each with an uppercase letter. End some sentences with periods and some with exclamation marks. Describe each situation.

68 CD-4339 Grammar Rules! Grades 5–6

RW: Answers will vary. DB: Answers will vary.

Page 69

You, You, You — subject of imperative sentences

A sentence that tells you what to do or gives you a command is called an imperative sentence. Most imperative sentences end with periods. An imperative sentence looks like a complete predicate. The complete subject is *you. You* is implied, which means that since the speaker is talking to you, it is understood that *you* is the subject, even though the word *you* isn't always written.

Underline the complete predicates. Circle the simple predicates.

(Brush) your teeth after every meal.
(Turn) off the television so you can get ready for bed.
(Call) me as soon as you arrive.
Don't (bring) food into your bedroom.
(Put) the return address in the upper, left corner of the envelope.
(Drink) plenty of water so you won't get dehydrated.

Change the interrogative sentences to imperative sentences.

Will you pass the salt and pepper?
Pass the salt and pepper.
Can you write Audrey a thank-you note this afternoon?
Write Audrey a thank-you note this afternoon.
Will you read the book and turn in a report by Monday?
Read the book and turn in a report by Monday.

Review Work
Change one imperative sentence from the top of the page to an interrogative sentence.

Draft Book
Write 10 imperative sentences. End each sentence with a period.

CD-4339 Grammar Rules! Grades 5–6 **69**

RW: Answers will vary. DB: Answers will vary.

Page 70

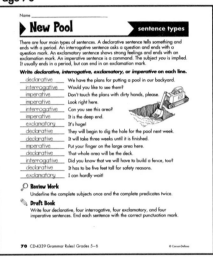

New Pool — sentence types

There are four main types of sentences. A declarative sentence tells something and ends with a period. An interrogative sentence asks a question and ends with a question mark. An exclamatory sentence shows strong feelings and ends with an exclamation mark. An imperative sentence is a command. The subject *you* is implied. It usually ends in a period, but can end in an exclamation mark.

Write *declarative, interrogative, exclamatory,* or *imperative* on each line.

declarative — We have the plans for putting a pool in our backyard.
interrogative — Would you like to see them?
imperative — Don't touch the plans with dirty hands, please.
imperative — Look right here.
interrogative — Can you see this area?
imperative — It is the deep end?
exclamatory — It's huge!
declarative — They will begin to dig the hole for the pool next week.
declarative — It will take three weeks until it is finished.
imperative — Put your finger on the large area here.
declarative — That whole area will be the deck.
interrogative — Did you know that we will have to build a fence, too?
declarative — It has to be five feet tall for safety reasons.
exclamatory — I can hardly wait!

Review Work
Underline the complete subjects once and the complete predicates twice.

Draft Book
Write four declarative, four interrogative, four exclamatory, and four imperative sentences. End each sentence with the correct punctuation mark.

70 CD-4339 Grammar Rules! Grades 5–6

RW: Underline we, you, (you), (you), you, it, it, they, it, (you), that whole area, you, it, and I once. Underline have the plans for putting a pool in our backyard; would like to see them; don't touch the plans with dirty hands, please; look right here; can see this area; is the deep end; 's huge; will begin to dig the hole for the pool next week; will take three weeks until it is finished; put your finger on the large area here, will be the deck; did know that we will have to build a fence, too; has to be five feet tall for safety reasons; and can hardly wait twice. **DB: Answers will vary.**

Answer Key

Page 71

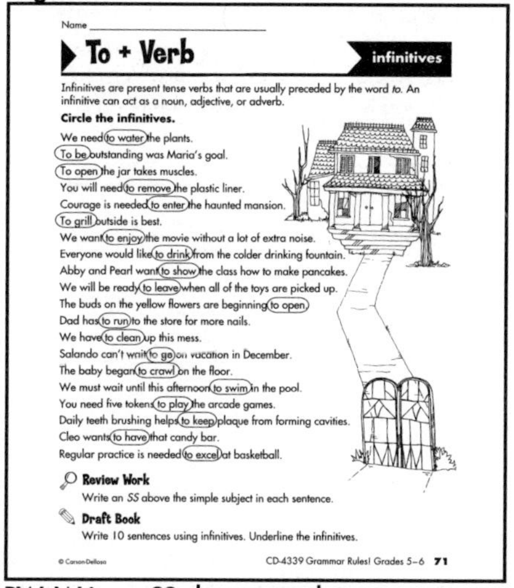

Name ____________

To + Verb — infinitives

Infinitives are present tense verbs that are usually preceded by the word *to*. An infinitive can act as a noun, adjective, or adverb.

Circle the infinitives.

We need to water the plants.
To be outstanding was Maria's goal.
To open the jar takes muscles.
You will need to remove the plastic liner.
Courage is needed to enter the haunted mansion.
To grill outside is best.
We want to enjoy the movie without a lot of extra noise.
Everyone would like to drink from the colder drinking fountain.
Abby and Pearl want to show the class how to make pancakes.
We will be ready to leave when all of the toys are picked up.
The buds on the yellow flowers are beginning to open.
Dad has to run to the store for more nails.
We have to clean up this mess.
Salando can't wait to go on vacation in December.
The baby began to crawl on the floor.
We must wait until this afternoon to swim in the pool.
You need five tokens to play the arcade games.
Daily teeth brushing helps to keep plaque from forming cavities.
Cleo wants to have that candy bar.
Regular practice is needed to excel at basketball.

Review Work
Write an *SS* above the simple subject in each sentence.

Draft Book
Write 10 sentences using infinitives. Underline the infinitives.

© Carson-Dellosa — CD-4339 Grammar Rules! Grades 5–6 **71**

RW: Write an SS above we, to be, to open, you, courage, to grill, we, everyone, Abby, Pearl, we, buds, Dad, we, Salando, baby, we, you, brushing, Cleo, and practice. DB: Answers will vary.

Page 72

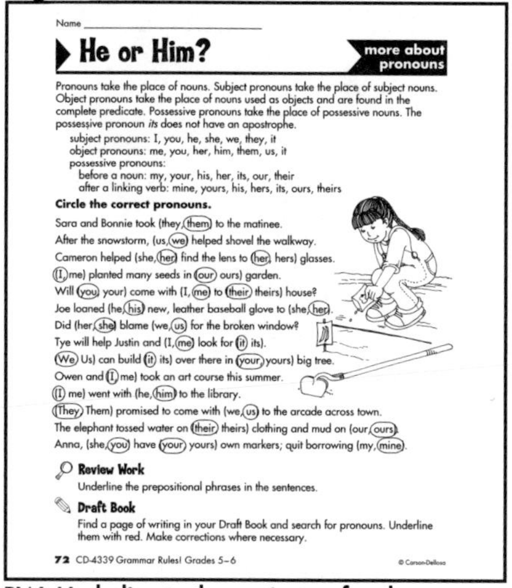

Name ____________

He or Him? — more about pronouns

Pronouns take the place of nouns. Subject pronouns take the place of subject nouns. Object pronouns take the place of nouns used as objects and are found in the complete predicate. Possessive pronouns take the place of possessive nouns. The possessive pronoun *its* does not have an apostrophe.

subject pronouns: I, you, he, she, we, they, it
object pronouns: me, you, her, him, them, us, it
possessive pronouns:
before a noun: my, your, his, her, its, our, their
after a linking verb: mine, yours, his, hers, its, ours, theirs

Circle the correct pronouns.

Sara and Bonnie took (they, them) to the matinee.
After the snowstorm, (us, we) helped shovel the walkway.
Cameron helped (she, her) find the lens to (her, hers) glasses.
(I, me) planted many seeds in (our, ours) garden.
Will (you, your) come with (I, me) to (their, theirs) house?
Joe loaned (he, his) new, leather baseball glove to (she, her).
Did (her, she) blame (we, us) for the broken window?
Tye will help Justin and (I, me) look for (it, its).
(We, Us) can build (it, its) over there in (your, yours) big tree.
Owen and (I, me) took an art course this summer.
(I, me) went with (he, him) to the library.
(They, Them) promised to come with (we, us) to the arcade across town.
The elephant tossed water on (their, theirs) clothing and mud on (our, ours).
Anna, (she, you) have (your, yours) own markers; quit borrowing (my, mine).

Review Work
Underline the prepositional phrases in the sentences.

Draft Book
Find a page of writing in your Draft Book and search for pronouns. Underline them with red. Make corrections where necessary.

72 CD-4339 Grammar Rules! Grades 5–6 — © Carson-Dellosa

RW: Underline to the matinee, after the snowstorm, to her glasses, in our garden, with me, to their house, to her, for the broken window, for it, over there, in your big tree, with him, to the library, to come, with us, to the arcade, across town, on their clothing, and on ours. DB: Answers will vary.

Page 73

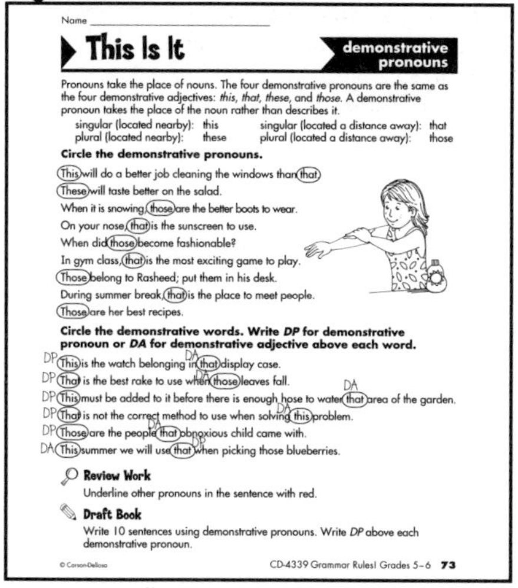

Name ____________

This Is It — demonstrative pronouns

Pronouns take the place of nouns. The four demonstrative pronouns are the same as the four demonstrative adjectives: *this, that, these,* and *those*. A demonstrative pronoun takes the place of the noun rather than describes it.

singular (located nearby): this — singular (located a distance away): that
plural (located nearby): these — plural (located a distance away): those

Circle the demonstrative pronouns.

This will do a better job cleaning the windows than that.
These will taste better on the salad.
When it is snowing, those are the better boots to wear.
On your nose, that is the sunscreen to use.
When did those become fashionable?
In gym class, that is the most exciting game to play.
Those belong to Rasheed; put them in his desk.
During summer break, that is the place to meet people.
Those are her best recipes.

Circle the demonstrative words. Write *DP* for demonstrative pronoun or *DA* for demonstrative adjective above each word.

DP This is the watch belonging in DA that display case.
DP That is the best rake to use when DA those leaves fall.
DP This must be added to it before there is enough hose to water DA that area of the garden.
DP That is not the correct method to use when solving DA this problem.
DP Those are the people DA that obnoxious child came with.
DA This summer we will use DP that when picking those blueberries.

Review Work
Underline other pronouns in the sentence with red.

Draft Book
Write 10 sentences using demonstrative pronouns. Write *DP* above each demonstrative pronoun.

© Carson-Dellosa — CD-4339 Grammar Rules! Grades 5–6 **73**

Page 73 (cont.)

RW: Underline it, your, them, his, her and we with red. DB: Answers will vary.

Page 74

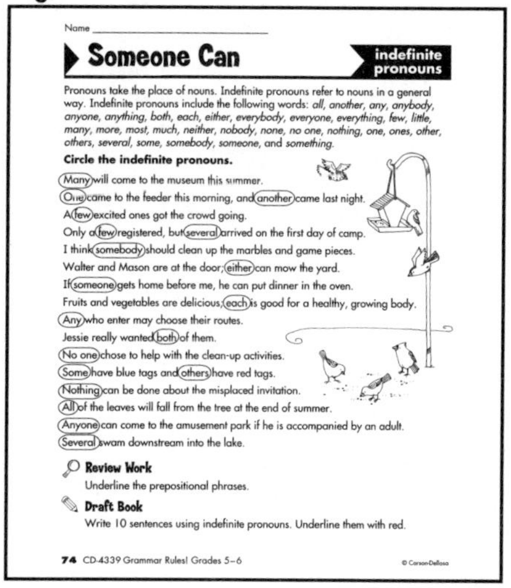

Name ____________

Someone Can — indefinite pronouns

Pronouns take the place of nouns. Indefinite pronouns refer to nouns in a general way. Indefinite pronouns include the following words: *all, another, any, anybody, anyone, anything, both, each, either, everybody, everyone, everything, few, little, many, more, most, much, neither, nobody, none, no one, nothing, one, ones, other, others, several, some, somebody, someone,* and *something*.

Circle the indefinite pronouns.

Many will come to the museum this summer.
One came to the feeder this morning, and another came last night.
A few excited ones got the crowd going.
Only a few registered, but several arrived on the first day of camp.
I think somebody should clean up the marbles and game pieces.
Walter and Mason are at the door; either can mow the yard.
If someone gets home before me, he can put dinner in the oven.
Fruits and vegetables are delicious; each is good for a healthy, growing body.
Any who enter may choose their routes.
Jessie really wanted both of them.
No one chose to help with the clean-up activities.
Some have blue tags and others have red tags.
Nothing can be done about the misplaced invitation.
All of the leaves will fall from the tree at the end of summer.
Anyone can come to the amusement park if he is accompanied by an adult.
Several swam downstream into the lake.

Review Work
Underline the prepositional phrases.

Draft Book
Write 10 sentences using indefinite pronouns. Underline them with red.

74 CD-4339 Grammar Rules! Grades 5–6 — © Carson-Dellosa

RW: Underline to the museum; to the feeder; on the first day; of camp; at the door; in the oven; for a healthy, growing body; of them; with the clean-up activities; about the misplaced invitation; of the leaves; from the tree; at the end of summer; to the amusement park; by an adult; and into the lake. DB: Answers will vary.

Page 75

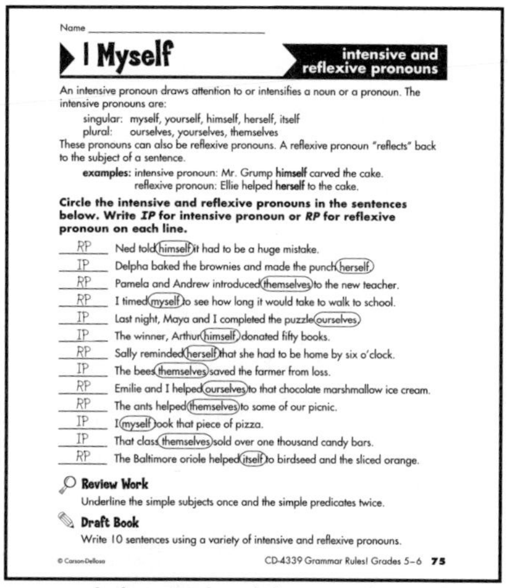

Name ____________

I Myself — intensive and reflexive pronouns

An intensive pronoun draws attention to or intensifies a noun or a pronoun. The intensive pronouns are:

singular: myself, yourself, himself, herself, itself
plural: ourselves, yourselves, themselves

These pronouns can also be reflexive pronouns. A reflexive pronoun "reflects" back to the subject of a sentence.

examples: intensive pronoun: Mr. Grump **himself** carved the cake.
reflexive pronoun: Ellie helped **herself** to the cake.

Circle the intensive and reflexive pronouns in the sentences below. Write *IP* for intensive pronoun or *RP* for reflexive pronoun on each line.

RP Ned told himself it had to be a huge mistake.
IP Delpha baked the brownies and made the punch herself.
RP Pamela and Andrew introduced themselves to the new teacher.
RP I timed myself to see how long it would take to walk to school.
IP Last night, Maya and I completed the puzzle ourselves.
IP The winner, Arthur himself, donated fifty books.
RP Sally reminded herself that she had to be home by six o'clock.
IP The bees themselves saved the farmer from loss.
RP Emilie and I helped ourselves to that chocolate marshmallow ice cream.
RP The ants helped themselves to some of our picnic.
IP I myself took that piece of pizza.
IP That class themselves sold over one thousand candy bars.
RP The Baltimore oriole helped itself to birdseed and the sliced orange.

Review Work
Underline the simple subjects once and the simple predicates twice.

Draft Book
Write 10 sentences using a variety of intensive and reflexive pronouns.

© Carson-Dellosa — CD-4339 Grammar Rules! Grades 5–6 **75**

RW: Underline Ned, Delpha, Pamela, Andrew, I, Maya, I, Arthur, Sally, bees, Emilie, I, ants, I, class, and Baltimore oriole once. Underline told, baked, introduced, timed, completed, donated, reminded, saved, helped, helped, took, sold, and helped twice.
DB: Answers will vary.

Page 76

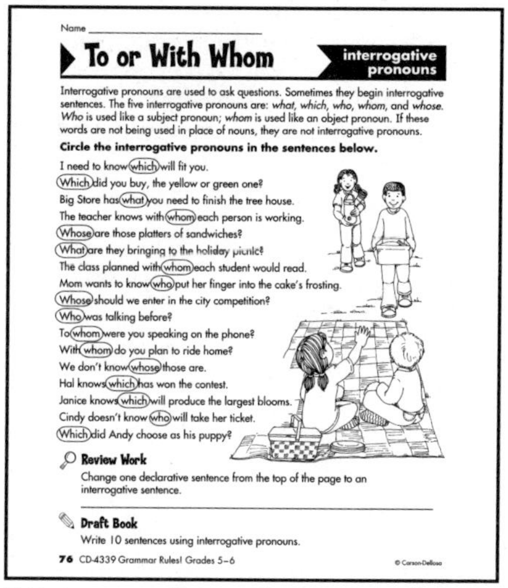

Name ____________

To or With Whom — interrogative pronouns

Interrogative pronouns are used to ask questions. Sometimes they begin interrogative sentences. The five interrogative pronouns are: *what, which, who, whom,* and *whose*. *Who* is used like a subject pronoun; *whom* is used like an object pronoun. If these words are not being used in place of nouns, they are not interrogative pronouns.

Circle the interrogative pronouns in the sentences below.

I need to know which will fit you.
Which did you buy, the yellow or green one?
Big Store has what you need to finish the tree house.
The teacher knows with whom each person is working.
Whose are those platters of sandwiches?
What are they bringing to the holiday picnic?
The class planned with whom each student would read.
Mom wants to know who put her finger into the cake's frosting.
Whose should we enter in the city competition?
Who was talking before?
To whom were you speaking on the phone?
With whom do you plan to ride home?
We don't know whose those are.
Hal knows which has won the contest.
Janice knows which will produce the largest blooms.
Cindy doesn't know who will take her ticket.
Which did Andy choose as his puppy?

Review Work
Change one declarative sentence from the top of the page to an interrogative sentence.

____

Draft Book
Write 10 sentences using interrogative pronouns.

76 CD-4339 Grammar Rules! Grades 5–6 — © Carson-Dellosa

RW: Answers will vary. DB: Answers will vary.

Page 77

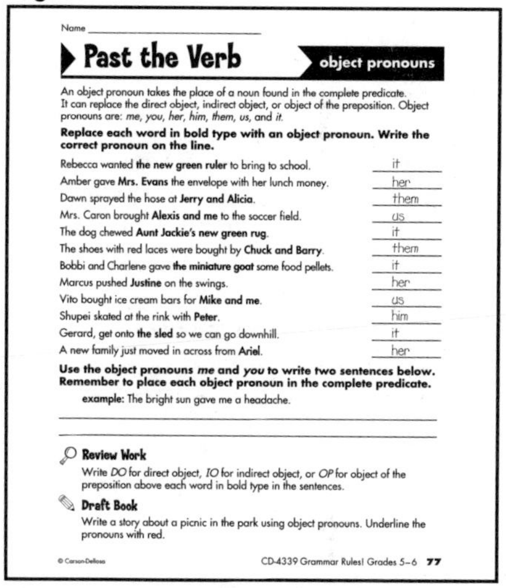

Name ____________

Past the Verb — object pronouns

An object pronoun takes the place of a noun found in the complete predicate. It can replace the direct object, indirect object, or object of the preposition. Object pronouns are: *me, you, her, him, them, us,* and *it*.

Replace each word in bold type with an object pronoun. Write the correct pronoun on the line.

Rebecca wanted **the new green ruler** to bring to school. — it
Amber gave **Mrs. Evans** the envelope with her lunch money. — her
Dawn sprayed the hose at **Jerry and Alicia**. — them
Mrs. Caron brought **Alexis and me** to the soccer field. — us
The dog chewed **Aunt Jackie's new green rug**. — it
The shoes with red laces were bought by **Chuck and Barry**. — them
Bobbi and Charlene gave **the miniature goat** some food pellets. — it
Marcus pushed **Justine** on the swings. — her
Vito bought ice cream bars for **Mike and me**. — us
Shupei skated at the rink with **Peter**. — him
Gerard, get onto **the sled** so we can go downhill. — it
A new family just moved in across from **Ariel**. — her

Use the object pronouns *me* and *you* to write two sentences below. Remember to place each object pronoun in the complete predicate.

example: The bright sun gave me a headache.

____

____

Review Work
Write *DO* for direct object, *IO* for indirect object, or *OP* for object of the preposition above each word in bold type in the sentences.

Draft Book
Write a story about a picnic in the park using object pronouns. Underline the pronouns with red.

© Carson-Dellosa — CD-4339 Grammar Rules! Grades 5–6 **77**

Answers will vary. RW: 1. DO 2. IO 3. OP 4. DO 5. DO 6. OP 7. IO 8. DO 9. OP 10. OP 11. OP 12. OP
DB: Answers will vary.

Page 78

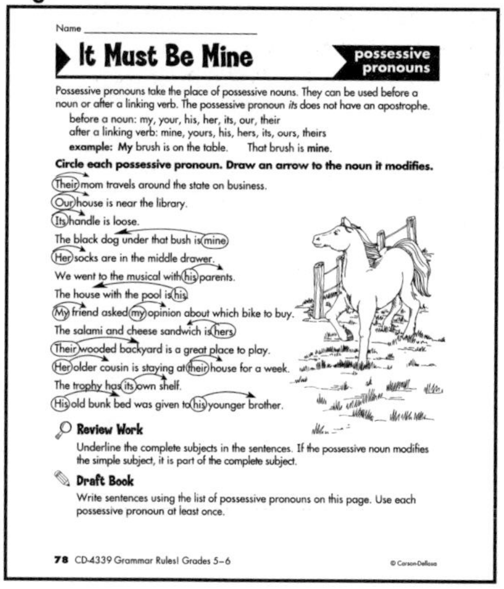

Name ____________

It Must Be Mine — possessive pronouns

Possessive pronouns take the place of possessive nouns. They can be used before a noun or after a linking verb. The possessive pronoun *its* does not have an apostrophe.

before a noun: my, your, his, her, its, our, their
after a linking verb: mine, yours, his, hers, its, ours, theirs
example: **My** brush is on the table. That brush is **mine**.

Circle each possessive pronoun. Draw an arrow to the noun it modifies.

Their mom travels around the state on business.
Our house is near the library.
Its handle is loose.
The black dog under that bush is mine.
Her socks are in the middle drawer.
We went to the musical with his parents.
The house with the pool is his.
My friend asked my opinion about which bike to buy.
The salami and cheese sandwich is hers.
Their wooded backyard is a great place to play.
Her older cousin is staying at their house for a week.
The trophy has its own shelf.
His old bunk bed was given to his younger brother.

Review Work
Underline the complete subjects in the sentences. If the possessive noun modifies the simple subject, it is part of the complete subject.

Draft Book
Write sentences using the list of possessive pronouns on this page. Use each possessive pronoun at least once.

78 CD-4339 Grammar Rules! Grades 5–6 — © Carson-Dellosa

Answer Key

Page 78 (cont.)

RW: Underline their mom, our house, its handle, the black dog under that bush, her socks, we, the house with the pool, my friend, the salami and cheese sandwich, their wooded backyard, her older cousin, the trophy, and his old bunk bed. DB: Answers will vary.

Page 79

Name ____________

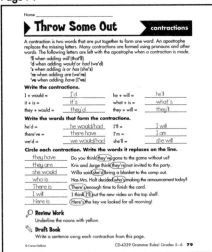

Throw Some Out — contractions

A contraction is two words that are put together to form one word. An apostrophe replaces the missing letters. Many contractions are formed using pronouns and other words. The following letters are left with the apostrophe when a contraction is made.

'll when adding *will* (that'll)
'd when adding *would* or *had* (we'd)
's when adding *is* or *has* (she's)
're when adding *are* (we're)
've when adding *have* (I've)

Write the contractions.

I + would =	I'd	he + will =	he'll
it + is =	it's	what + is =	what's
they + would =	they'd	they + will =	they'll

Write the words that form the contractions.

he'd =	he would/had	I'll =	I will
there've =	there have	I'm =	I am
we'd =	we would/had	she'll =	she will

Circle each contraction. Write the words it replaces on the line.

they have — Do you think they've gone to the game without us?
they are — Kris and Jorge think they're not invited to the party.
she would — Willa said she'd bring a blanket to the camp out.
who is — Has Mrs. Holt decided who's making the announcement today?
There is — There's enough time to finish the card.
I will — I think I'll put the new video on the top shelf.
Here is — Here's the key we looked for all morning!

Review Work
Underline the nouns with yellow.

Draft Book
Write a sentence using each contraction from this page.

© Carson-Dellosa CD-4339 Grammar Rules! Grades 5–6 79

RW: Underline game, Kris, Jorge, party, Willa, blanket, camp out, Mrs. Holt, announcement, time, card, video, shelf, key, and morning. DB: Answers will vary.

Page 80

Name ____________

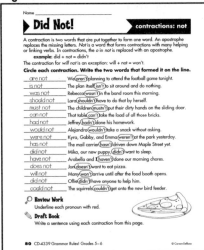

Did Not! — contractions: not

A contraction is two words that are put together to form one word. An apostrophe replaces the missing letters. *Not* is a word that forms contractions with many helping or linking verbs. In contractions, the *o* in *not* is replaced with an apostrophe.

example: did + not = didn't

The contraction for *will not* is an exception: will + not = won't.

Circle each contraction. Write the two words that formed it on the line.

are not — We aren't planning to attend the football game tonight.
is not — The plan itself isn't to sit around and do nothing.
was not — Rebecca wasn't in the band room this morning.
should not — Lara shouldn't have to do that by herself.
must not — The children mustn't put their dirty hands on the sliding door.
can not — That table can't take the load of all those bricks.
had not — Jeffrey hadn't done his homework.
would not — Alejandro wouldn't take a snack without asking.
were not — Kyra, Gabby, and Emma weren't at the park yesterday.
has not — The mail carrier hasn't driven down Maple Street yet.
did not — Mika, our new puppy, didn't want to sleep.
have not — Arabella and I haven't done our morning chores.
does not — Jon doesn't want to eat pizza.
will not — Many won't arrive until after the food booth opens.
did not — Ollie didn't have anyone to help him.
could not — The squirrels couldn't get onto the new bird feeder.

Review Work
Underline each pronoun with red.

Draft Book
Write a sentence using each contraction from this page.

80 CD-4339 Grammar Rules! Grades 5–6 © Carson-Dellosa

RW: Underline we, itself, this, that, herself, their, that, those, his, our, I, our, many, anyone, and him with red.
DB: Answers will vary.

Page 81

Name ____________

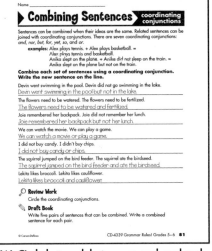

Combining Sentences — coordinating conjunctions

Sentences can be combined when their ideas are the same. Related sentences can be joined with coordinating conjunctions. There are seven coordinating conjunctions: *and, nor, but, for, yet, so,* and *or.*

examples: Alex plays tennis. + Alex plays basketball. =
Alex plays tennis and basketball.
Anika slept on the plane. + Anika did not sleep on the train. =
Anika slept on the plane but not on the train.

Combine each set of sentences using a coordinating conjunction. Write the new sentence on the line.

Devin went swimming in the pool. Devin did not go swimming in the lake.
Devin went swimming in the pool but not in the lake.
The flowers need to be watered. The flowers need to be fertilized.
The flowers need to be watered and fertilized.
Joie remembered her backpack. Joie did not remember her lunch.
Joie remembered her backpack but not her lunch.
We can watch the movie. We can play a game.
We can watch a movie or play a game.
I did not buy candy. I didn't buy chips.
I did not buy candy or chips.
The squirrel jumped on the bird feeder. The squirrel ate the birdseed.
The squirrel jumped on the bird feeder and ate the birdseed.
Lekita likes broccoli. Lekita likes cauliflower.
Lekita likes broccoli and cauliflower.

Review Work
Circle the coordinating conjunctions.

Draft Book
Write five pairs of sentences that can be combined. Write a combined sentence for each pair.

© Carson-Dellosa CD-4339 Grammar Rules! Grades 5–6 81

RW: Circle but, and, but, or, or, and, and and. DB: Answers will vary.

Page 82

Name ____________

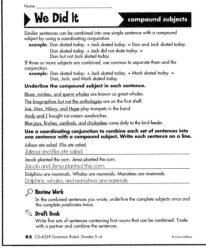

We Did It — compound subjects

Similar sentences can be combined into one simple sentence with a compound subject by using a coordinating conjunction.

example: Dan skated today. + Jack skated today. = Dan and Jack skated today.
Dan skated today. + Jack did not skate today. =
Dan but not Jack skated today.

If three or more subjects are combined, use commas to separate them and the conjunction.

example: Dan skated today. + Jack skated today. + Mark skated today. =
Dan, Jack, and Mark skated today.

Underline the compound subject in each sentence.

Blues, minkes, and sperm whales are known as great whales.
The biographies but not the anthologies are on the first shelf.
Joe, Max, Hilary, and Hope play trumpets in the band.
Andy and I bought ice-cream sandwiches.
Blue jays, finches, cardinals, and chickadees come daily to the bird feeder.

Use a coordinating conjunction to combine each set of sentences into one sentence with a compound subject. Write each sentence on a line.

Julissa ate salad. Elia ate salad.
Julissa and Elia ate salad.
Jacob planted the corn. Jerez planted the corn.
Jacob and Jerez planted the corn.
Dolphins are mammals. Whales are mammals. Manatees are mammals.
Dolphins, whales, and manatees are mammals.

Review Work
In the combined sentences you wrote, underline the complete subjects once and the complete predicates twice.

Draft Book
Write five sets of sentences containing first nouns that can be combined. Trade with a partner and combine the sentences.

82 CD-4339 Grammar Rules! Grades 5–6 © Carson-Dellosa

RW: Underline Julissa and Elia; Jacob and Jerez; and dolphins, whales and manatees once. Underline ate salad, planted the corn, and are mammals twice. DB: Answers will vary.

Page 83

Name ____________

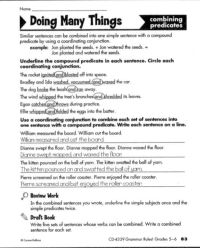

Doing Many Things — combining predicates

Similar sentences can be combined into one simple sentence with a compound predicate by using a coordinating conjunction.

example: Jon planted the seeds. + Jon watered the seeds. =
Jon planted and watered the seeds.

Underline the compound predicate in each sentence. Circle each coordinating conjunction.

The rocket ignited and blasted off into space.
Bradley and Ida washed, vacuumed, and waxed the car.
The dog broke the leash and ran away.
The wind whipped the tree's branches and shredded its leaves.
Egan catches and throws during practice.
Ellie whipped and folded the eggs into the batter.

Use a coordinating conjunction to combine each set of sentences into one sentence with a compound predicate. Write each sentence on a line.

William measured the board. William cut the board.
William measured and cut the board.
Dianne swept the floor. Dianne mopped the floor. Dianne waxed the floor.
Dianne swept, mopped, and waxed the floor.
The kitten pounced on the ball of yarn. The kitten swatted the ball of yarn.
The kitten pounced on and swatted the ball of yarn.
Pierre screamed on the roller coaster. Pierre enjoyed the roller coaster.
Pierre screamed and/but enjoyed the roller coaster.

Review Work
In the combined sentences you wrote, underline the simple subjects once and the simple predicates twice.

Draft Book
Write five sets of sentences whose verbs can be combined. Write a combined sentence for each set.

© Carson-Dellosa CD-4339 Grammar Rules! Grades 5–6 83

Page 83 (cont.)

RW: Underline William, Dianne, kitten, and Pierre once. Underline measured, swept, mopped, waxed, pounced, swatted, screamed, and enjoyed twice. DB: Answers will vary.

Page 84

Name ____________

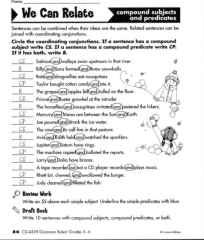

We Can Relate — compound subjects and predicates

Sentences can be combined when their ideas are the same. Related sentences can be joined with coordinating conjunctions.

Circle the coordinating conjunctions. If a sentence has a compound subject write *CS*. If a sentence has a compound predicate write *CP*. If it has both, write *B*.

CS — Salmon and walleye swim upstream in that river.
B — Billy and Sara formed and threw snowballs.
CS — Bats and dragonflies eat mosquitoes.
CP — Taylor bought cotton candy and ate it.
B — The grapes and apples fell and rolled on the floor.
CS — Prince and Buster growled at the intruder.
B — The horseflies and mosquitoes irritated and pestered the hikers.
CS — Mercury and Venus are between the Sun and Earth.
CP — Joe poured and drank the ice water.
CS — The cow and its calf live in that pasture.
B — Avis and Edith held and watched the sparklers.
CS — Jupiter and Saturn have rings.
CP — The machine copied and collated the reports.
CS — Larry and Dalia have braces.
B — A tape recorder but not a CD player records and plays music.
CP — Rhett bit, chewed, and swallowed the burger.
CP — Judy cleaned and filleted the fish.

Review Work
Write an *SS* above each simple subject. Underline the simple predicates with blue.

Draft Book
Write 10 sentences with compound subjects, compound predicates, or both.

84 CD-4339 Grammar Rules! Grades 5–6 © Carson-Dellosa

RW: Write an SS above salmon, walleye, Billy, Sara, bats, dragonflies, Taylor, grapes, apples, Prince, Buster, horseflies, mosquitoes, Mercury, Venus, Joe, cow, calf, Avis, Edith, Jupiter, Saturn, machine, Larry, Dalia, tape recorder, player, Rhett, and Judy. Underline swim, formed, threw, eat, bought, ate, fell, rolled, growled, irritated, pestered, are, poured, drank, live, held, watched, have, copied, collated, have, records, plays, bit, chewed, swallowed, cleaned, and filleted with blue. DB: Answers will vary.

Page 85

Name ____________

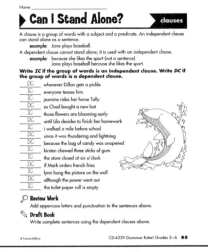

Can I Stand Alone? — clauses

A clause is a group of words with a subject and a predicate. An independent clause can stand alone as a sentence.

example: Jane plays baseball.

A dependent clause cannot stand alone; it is used with an independent clause.

example: because she likes the sport (not a sentence)
Jane plays baseball because she likes the sport.

Write *IC* if the group of words is an independent clause. Write *DC* if the group of words is a dependent clause.

DC — whenever Dillon gets a pickle
IC — everyone teases him
IC — jasmine rides her horse Tally
DC — so Chad bought a new bat
IC — those flowers are blooming early
DC — until Lila decides to finish her homework
IC — i walked a mile before school
DC — since it was thundering and lightning
DC — because the bag of candy was unopened
IC — kirsten chewed three sticks of gum
IC — the store closed at six o'clock
DC — if Mark orders french fries
IC — lynn hung the picture on the wall
DC — although the power went out
IC — the toilet-paper roll is empty

Review Work
Add uppercase letters and punctuation to the sentences above.

Draft Book
Write complete sentences using the dependent clauses above.

© Carson-Dellosa CD-4339 Grammar Rules! Grades 5–6 85

RW: Add uppercase letters and punctuation to sentences. DB: Answers will vary.

Answer Key

Page 86

Name ____________

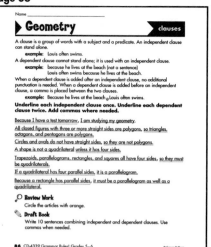

Geometry — clauses

A clause is a group of words with a subject and a predicate. An independent clause can stand alone.

example: Louis often swims.

A dependent clause cannot stand alone; it is used with an independent clause.

example: because he lives at the beach (not a sentence)
Louis often swims because he lives at the beach.

When a dependent clause is added after an independent clause, no additional punctuation is needed. When a dependent clause is added before an independent clause, a comma is placed between the two clauses.

example: Because he lives at the beach, Louis often swims.

Underline each independent clause once. Underline each dependent clause twice. Add commas where needed.

Because I have a test tomorrow, I am studying my geometry.
All closed figures with three or more straight sides are polygons, so triangles, octagons, and pentagons are polygons.
Circles and ovals do not have straight sides, so they are not polygons.
A shape is not a quadrilateral unless it has four sides.
Trapezoids, parallelograms, rectangles, and squares all have four sides, so they must be quadrilaterals.
If a quadrilateral has four parallel sides, it is a parallelogram.
Because a rectangle has parallel sides, it must be a parallelogram as well as a quadrilateral.

Review Work
Circle the articles with orange.

Draft Book
Write 10 sentences combining independent and dependent clauses. Use commas when needed.

86 CD-4339 Grammar Rules! Grades 5–6 © Carson-Dellosa

RW: Circle each a. DB: Answers will vary.

Page 87

Name ____________

Just a Piece — phrases and clauses

A phrase is a group of words that does not have a subject and predicate. A clause is a group of words with a subject and a predicate. An independent clause can stand alone. A dependent clause cannot stand alone.

Write *P* if the group of words is a phrase. Write *IC* if the group of words is an independent clause. Write *DC* if the group of words is a dependent clause.

P with Tom and me
IC Doug walks
DC whenever the news comes on television
P running and jumping in the leaves
P around nine o'clock
IC Jill likes drawing
P is great at editing
DC so that he can get his work done
P shimmering and sparkling in the sun
IC sea turtles swim many miles
P the open bag of potato chips
P little striped fish
DC although I knew the material
P crashing through the woods
DC if Olive wins one more competition
DC after Jean missed the bus
IC this pen works
IC Jeff mows the lawn

Review Work
Add uppercase letters and punctuation to the independent clauses above.

Draft Book
Use the phrases and dependent clauses to write complete sentences.

© Carson-Dellosa CD-4339 Grammar Rules! Grades 5–6 87

RW: Add uppercase letters and punctuation to independent clauses. DB: Answers will vary.

Page 88

Name ____________

Stop the Run — independent clauses and conjunctions

When two independent clauses are written together, they create a run-on sentence. Two related independent clauses can be joined into one sentence with a comma and coordinating conjunction. There are seven coordinating conjunctions: *and, nor, but, for, yet, so,* and *or.*

example: Jasmine needs a nap, or she may fall asleep.
subject predicate conjunction subject predicate

Write an *SS* above each simple subject and underline each simple predicate.

The bluebird swooped down, but it missed the grasshopper.
Val read the ingredients on the ice-cream package, but she didn't find "milk" anywhere.
We are going skiing, and I am bringing my scarf.
Frannie gave the dog a treat, yet it is still barking.
Alvie has a test tomorrow, so she is planning to study tonight.
I knitted the scarf for Dana, but she didn't like it.
Lola didn't clean her room, so she can't leave right now.
You can choose swimming for a physical education class, or you can choose gymnastics.
The phone is ringing, yet no one has answered it.
Lola's watch is under warranty, yet the store refuses to fix it.
You can clear the table, or I can do it.
Fortoula and Melina love strawberries, so they are going to pick some tomorrow.

Review Work
Circle the commas and coordinating conjunctions used to separate the independent clauses.

Draft Book
Write 10 sentences that join independent clauses with commas and conjunctions.

88 CD-4339 Grammar Rules! Grades 5–6 © Carson-Dellosa

RW: Circle but, but, and, yet, so, but, so, or, yet, yet, or, so, and the commas that come before them. DB: Answers will vary.

Page 89

Name ____________

One or Two? — independent clauses and conjunctions

When two independent clauses are written together, they create a run-on sentence. To correct a run-on, decide where the first sentence ends and the second begins. The clauses can remain in one sentence if they are separated by a comma and a coordinating conjunction. There are seven coordinating conjunctions: *and, nor, but, for, yet, so,* and *or.*

example: The stars were coming out the moon wasn't up yet. =
The stars were coming out, but the moon wasn't up yet.

Separate each run-on sentence with a comma and a conjunction. Rewrite the sentences correctly on the lines.

Hannah was exhausted she had to finish her homework.
Hannah was exhausted, but she had to finish her homework.

Tyrone saw that man drop his wallet he returned it to him.
Tyrone saw that man drop his wallet, so he returned it to him.

Is that box heavy is that box light?
Is that box heavy, or is that box light?

The rain came down in a torrent it flooded the driveway.
The rain came down in a torrent, and it flooded the driveway.

Kate kicked the ball hard she made the winning goal.
Kate kicked the ball hard, and she made the winning goal.

We could go to the movies we could go to the arcade.
We could go to the movies, or we could go to the arcade.

I have the hiccups I am getting a glass of water.
I have the hiccups, so I am getting a glass of water.

Review Work
Underline the complete subjects once and the complete predicates twice.

Draft Book
Write five sentences that join independent clauses with commas and conjunctions.

© Carson-Dellosa CD-4339 Grammar Rules! Grades 5–6 89

RW: Underline Hannah, she, Tyrone, he, that box, that box, the rain, it, Kate, she, we, we, I, and I once. Underline was exhausted, had to finish her homework, saw that man drop his wallet, returned it to him, is heavy, is light, came down in a torrent, flooded the driveway, kicked the ball hard, made the winning goal, could go to the movies, could go to the arcade, have the hiccups, and am getting a glass of water twice. DB: Answers will vary.

Page 90

Name ____________

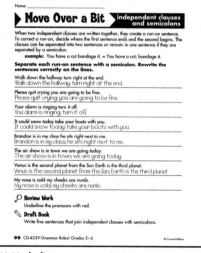

Move Over a Bit — independent clauses and semicolons

When two independent clauses are written together, they create a run-on sentence. To correct a run-on, decide where the first sentence ends and the second begins. The clauses can be separated into two sentences or remain in one sentence if they are separated by a semicolon.

example: You have a cut bandage it. = You have a cut; bandage it.

Separate each run-on sentence with a semicolon. Rewrite the sentences correctly on the lines.

Walk down the hallway turn right at the end.
Walk down the hallway; turn right at the end.

Please quit crying you are going to be fine.
Please quit crying; you are going to be fine.

Your alarm is ringing turn it off.
You alarm is ringing; turn it off.

It could snow today take your boots with you.
It could snow today; take your boots with you.

Brandon is in my class he sits right next to me.
Brandon is in my class; he sits right next to me.

The air show is in town we are going today.
The air show is in town; we are going today.

Venus is the second planet from the Sun Earth is the third planet.
Venus is the second planet from the Sun; Earth is the third planet.

My nose is cold my cheeks are numb.
My nose is cold; my cheeks are numb.

Review Work
Underline the pronouns with red.

Draft Book
Write five sentences that join independent clauses with semicolons.

90 CD-4339 Grammar Rules! Grades 5–6 © Carson-Dellosa

RW: Underline you, your, it, it, your, you, my, he, me, we, my, and my with red. DB: Answers will vary.

Page 91

Name ____________

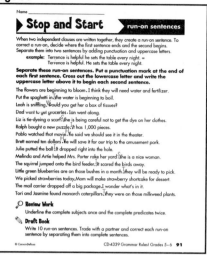

Stop and Start — run-on sentences

When two independent clauses are written together, they create a run-on sentence. To correct a run-on, decide where the first sentence ends and the second begins. Separate them into two sentences by adding punctuation and uppercase letters.

example: Terrence is helpful he sets the table every night. =
Terrence is helpful. He sets the table every night.

Separate these run-on sentences. Put a punctuation mark at the end of each first sentence. Cross out the lowercase letter and write the uppercase letter above it to begin each second sentence.

The flowers are beginning to bloom. I think they will need water and fertilizer.
Put the spaghetti in. The water is beginning to boil.
Leah is sniffling. Would you get her a box of tissues?
Dad went to get groceries. Ian went along.
Liz is tie-dyeing a scarf. She is being careful not to get the dye on her clothes.
Ralph bought a new puzzle. It has 1,000 pieces.
Pablo watched that movie. He said we should see it in the theater.
Brett earned ten dollars. He will save it for our trip to the amusement park.
Julie putted the ball. It dropped right into the hole.
Melinda and Artie helped Mrs. Porter rake her yard. She is a nice woman.
The squirrel jumped onto the bird feeder. It scared the birds away.
Little green blueberries are on those bushes in a month. They will be ready to pick.
We picked strawberries today. Mom will make strawberry shortcake for dessert.
The mail carrier dropped off a big package. I wonder what's in it.
Tori and Jasmine found monarch caterpillars. They were on those milkweed plants.

Review Work
Underline the complete subjects once and the complete predicates twice.

Draft Book
Write 10 run-on sentences. Trade with a partner and correct each run-on sentence by separating them into complete sentences.

© Carson-Dellosa CD-4339 Grammar Rules! Grades 5–6 91

RW: Underline the flowers, I, (you), the water, Leah, you, Dad, Ian, Liz, she, Ralph, it, Pablo, he, Brett, he, Julie, it, Melinda and Artie, she, the squirrel, it, little green blueberries, in a month they, we, Mom, the mail carrier, I, Tori and Jasmine, and they once. Underline are beginning to bloom, think they will need water and fertilizer, put the spaghetti in, is beginning to boil, is sniffling, would get her a box of tissues, went to get groceries, went along, is tie-dying a scarf, is being careful not to get the dye on her clothes, bought a new puzzle, has 1,000 pieces, watched that movie, said we should see it in the theater, earned ten dollars, will save it for our trip to the amusement park, putted the ball, dropped right into the hole, helped Mrs. Porter rake her yard, is a nice woman, jumped onto the bird feeder, scared the birds away, are on those bushes, will be ready to pick, picked strawberries today, will make strawberry shortcake for dessert, dropped off a big package, wonder what's in it, found monarch caterpillars, and were on those milkweed plants twice. DB: Answers will vary.

Page 92

Name ____________

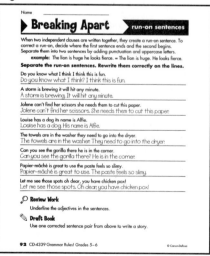

Breaking Apart — run-on sentences

When two independent clauses are written together, they create a run-on sentence. To correct a run-on, decide where the first sentence ends and the second begins. Separate them into two sentences by adding punctuation and uppercase letters.

example: The lion is huge he looks fierce. = The lion is huge. He looks fierce.

Separate the run-on sentences. Rewrite them correctly on the lines.

Do you know what I think I think this is fun.
Do you know what I think? I think this is fun.

A storm is brewing it will hit any minute.
A storm is brewing. It will hit any minute.

Jolene can't find her scissors she needs them to cut this paper.
Jolene can't find her scissors. She needs them to cut this paper.

Louise has a dog its name is Alfie.
Louise has a dog. His name is Alfie.

The towels are in the washer they need to go into the dryer.
The towels are in the washer. They need to go into the dryer.

Can you see the gorilla there he is in the corner.
Can you see the gorilla there? He is in the corner.

Papier-mâché is great to use the paste feels so slimy.
Papier-mâché is great to use. The paste feels so slimy.

Let me see those spots oh dear, you have chicken pox!
Let me see those spots. Oh dear, you have chicken pox!

Review Work
Underline the adjectives in the sentences.

Draft Book
Use one corrected sentence pair from above to write a story.

92 CD-4339 Grammar Rules! Grades 5–6 © Carson-Dellosa

RW: Underline fun, brewing, any, her, this, great, so slimy, and those. DB: Answers will vary.

Page 93: Answers will vary.
Page 94: Answers will vary.

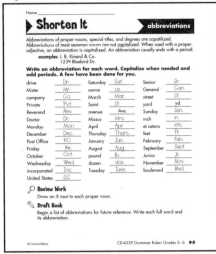

RW: Draw an X next to Monday, December, Friday, October, Wednesday, United States, Saturday, March, April, Thursday, January, August, Tuesday, Sunday, February, September, and November. DB: Answers will vary.

Page 96

RW: Write an SS above I, we, (you), I, something, you, that, I, I, and (you). DB: Answers will vary.

Page 97

RW: Circle package, clothing, letter, and Town. DB: Answers will vary.

Page 98

RW: Write two of the following: Sun., Aug. 18, 1991; Wed., Feb. 26; Oct. 11, 1973; Dec. 30; and Tues., June 29. DB: Answers will vary.

Page 99

RW: Circle a, the, the, and a with orange. DB: Answers will vary.

Page 100

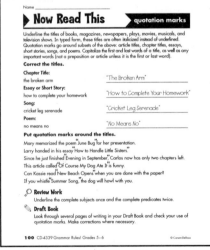

RW: Circle June Bug, dog, and dog. DB: Answers will vary.

Page 101

RW: Draw an X next to Sen. J. K. Post, Dr. Heath, Henry, Jesse, Jamal, and Ryan. DB: Answers will vary.

Page 102

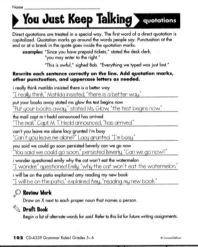

RW: Draw an X next to Matilda, Ms. Glow, Capt. M. T. Head, Lacy, Beverly, Emily, and Amy. DB: Answers will vary.

Page 103

RW: Draw an X next to Pippa, Mike B. Helmet, Sadie, Ramsey, Majaa, Merle, Mom, Jon, and Mr. Rich. Draw a triangle above America and Antarctica. DB: Answers will vary.